# The Vimalakirti Sutra

W9-AWB-532

TRANSLATIONS FROM THE ASIAN CLASSICS

TRANSLATIONS FROM THE ASIAN CLASSICS

EDITORIAL BOARD
Wm. Theodore de Bary, Chairman
Paul Anderer
Irene Bloom
Donald Keene
George A. Saliba
Haruo Shirane
David D. W. Wang
Burton Watson
Philip B. Yampolsky

# The Vimalakirti Sutra

*Translated by Burton Watson*
*from the Chinese version by Kumarajiva*

Columbia University Press NEW YORK

Columbia University Press

Publishers Since 1893

New York     Chichester, West Sussex

Copyright © 1997 Columbia University Press

All rights reserved

Library of Congress Cataloging-in-Publication Data

Tripiṭaka. Sūtrapiṭaka. Vimalakīrtinirdeśa. English.

    The Vimalakirti Sutra / translated by Burton Watson from the
Chinese version by Kumarajiva.

      p.   cm. — (Translations from the Asian classics)

    ISBN 0–231–10656–4 (cloth) — ISBN 0–231–10657–2 (paper)

    I. Watson, Burton, 1925–  .  II. Series.

BQ2212.E5W66   1996

294.3'85—dc20                         96–18578

Casebound editions of Columbia University Press books are printed
on permanent and durable acid-free paper.

Printed in the United States of America

Designed by Lisa Force

c 10 9 8 7 6 5 4 3 2

p 10 9 8 7 6 5 4 3 2 1

*To the memory of my friend and colleague*
*Barbara Stoler Miller*
*1940–1993*

# CONTENTS

# TRANSLATOR'S NOTE

The Kumarajiva translation of the Vimalakirti Sutra, with its elegant and neatly balanced phrases, has exercised an enormous influence in China and the other countries within the Chinese cultural sphere. Except for a rather murky passage at the end of chapter 4, it reads right along in beautifully concise classical Chinese, and it is for the most part free of the tedious repetitions that make some of the other Mahayana sutras a chore to read. In philosophical depth and brilliance of language it rivals the *Chuang Tzu*, the collected writings of the early Chinese Taoist philosopher Chuang Chou, and it is significant that both works enjoyed particular popularity among the literary-minded gentry of the Six Dynasties period.

Some years ago I had the pleasure of translating Chuang Tzu into English, a project that resulted in the publication of *The Complete Works of Chuang Tzu* by Columbia University Press in 1968. For many years I also had it in mind to undertake an English translation of Kumarajiva's version of the Vimalakirti Sutra, a work that in many ways so closely resembles the *Chuang Tzu*. I had hoped to do so in collaboration with Professor Yoshito S. Hakeda, my colleague at Columbia University and the translator of *The Awakening of Faith* and the writings of Kūkai, but his untimely death brought those hopes to an end. The present work represents a belated realization of my plans. The translation is dedicated to the memory of another colleague of mine at Columbia University and Barnard, Professor Barbara Stoler Miller, with whom I taught many classes in Asian literature, the one person to whom I would most like to have shown this translation.

Like my earlier translation of the Lotus Sutra, the present volume is intended primarily for readers who have no special background in Buddhist studies. Sanskrit names and terms have been romanized in a form that differs slightly from the standard form used in works intended for specialists; standard romanization for all such words may be found in the glossary at the back of the book. In giving English equivalents of Buddhist terminology, I have wherever possible followed the same forms as those used in my Lotus Sutra translation.

Readers who wish more detailed information about such terminology and about the thought and background of the Vimalakirti Sutra should consult the translation by Robert A. F. Thurman, *The Holy Teaching of Vimalakīrti* (University Park and London: The Pennsylvania State University Press, 1979). The translation is done from a Tibetan version of the text that differs somewhat from that of Kumarajiva, but it contains extensive notes and glossary entries. For a still more specialized and exhaustive treatment of the text, one may consult the French translation, done from the Tibetan and Hsüan-tsang's Chinese version, by Étienne Lamotte, *L'Enseignement de Vimalakīrti* (Louvain, 1962), or the English translation of Lamotte's volume, *The Teaching of Vimalakīrti*, translated by Sara Boin (London: The Pali Text Society, 1976). For another English version of Kumarajiva's Chinese translation of the sutra, see Charles Luk, *The Vimalakirti Nirdesa Sutra* (Boston: Shambhala, 1990). All the above works have been of great assistance to me in making my own version.

I have also consulted with profit the Japanese translations from the sutra in Mushanokōji Saneatsu's *Yuimagyō* (Tokyo: Daitō shuppansha, 1934), the excellent modern language translation by Ishida Mizumaro, *Yuimagyō* (Tokyo: Tōyō bunko #67, 1966); the more recent but less helpful version by Takasaki Jikidō, *Yuimakitsu shosetsu kyō* (Tokyo: Shin Kokuyaku daizōkyō, Daizō shuppan kabushiki kaisha, 1993); and the modern

Japanese language translation by Nagao Gadjin, done from the Tibetan version of the text, *Yuimagyō* (Tokyo: Daijō butten #7, rev. ed., Chūōkōronsha, 1992).

There are few important textual variants in the Kumarajiva Chinese version of the sutra. Those that seriously affect the meaning are indicated in my footnotes to the translation.

Among the numerous sutras or sacred texts of Mahayana Buddhism, some, such as the Lotus Sutra, are noted for the majestic scale and sweep of their narrative and their devotional chapters, others like the Heart Sutra for their extreme conciseness, and still others such as the Amidist sutras for their vivid depictions of the Pure Land or paradise of a particular Buddha. The Vimalakirti Sutra, one of the most famous and influential works of the Mahayana canon, is outstanding for the eloquent and orderly manner in which it expounds the basic tenets of Mahayana, the liveliness of its episodes, and its frequent touches of humor, these last a rarity in a religious work of this type. The Vimalakirti Sutra is also unusual in that its central figure is not a Buddha or Buddhas but a wealthy townsman of Shakyamuni's time, Vimalakirti, who in his religious understanding and practice epitomizes the ideal lay believer. For this reason, and because of the sutra's remarkable literary appeal, it has enjoyed particular popularity among lay Buddhists in China, Japan, and the other Asian countries where Mahayana doctrines prevail and has exercised a marked influence on their literature and art. Highly regarded by nearly all branches of Mahayana Buddhism, it has held a place of particular importance in the Ch'an or Zen sect.

The Vimalakirti Sutra appears to be a product of the early years of the Mahayana movement, though just where, when, or by whom it was composed is unknown. The earliest Chinese translation, now lost, was done in 188 C.E., so the sutra must predate that year, originating probably around 100 C.E. It was translated into Chinese six more times, the last translation done by Hsüan-tsang in the years 627–648 C.E.. By far the most popular and influential Chinese translation is the sixth, done by the Central Asian scholar-monk Kumarajiva in 406 C.E., from which the present English version has been made.

The sutra was later translated into Tibetan, probably in the early eighth century, and also into Sogdian, Khotanese, Mongolian, and Manchu, these last in all likelihood being done from a Chinese or Tibetan translation of the work. The original Sanskrit text of the sutra was lost long ago, though brief quotations from it are preserved in other works.

The Sanskrit title of the text, *Vimalakīrti-nirdeśa-sūtra*, which is translated here as *Sutra on the Expositions of Vimalakirti*, clearly indicates that Vimalakirti is to be the principal propounder of the doctrine, with Shakyamuni Buddha playing a secondary role, while the sutra itself in its closing chapter offers an alternative title, *The Doctrine of the Emancipation Beyond Comprehension*. It is also sometimes referred to in Chinese as the *Cheng-ming ching*, Cheng-ming or "Pure Fame" being the Chinese translation of the name *Vimalakirti*. For convenience sake I have at most times referred to it simply as the Vimalakirti Sutra.

The sutra, which consists of fourteen chapters in Kumarajiva's Chinese translation, opens with a scene in the Amra Gardens in the city of Vaishali in northeastern India, where Shakyamuni Buddha is expounding the Law to a vast assembly of monks, nuns, bodhisattvas, and lay believers, as well as various gods and other nonhuman beings. Chapter 2 introduces the figure of Vimalakirti, a rich layman residing in Vaishali who in his daily life represents a paragon of Buddhist enlightenment and practice. In order to further his propagation of the Buddhist doctrine, he has made it appear that he is ill; when the ruler of the region, the officials, and other residents of the area call on him to inquire about his condition, he then utilizes the opportunity to lecture them on the sacred teachings.

Shakyamuni Buddha, learning of this situation, requests one after another of his ten major monk disciples to go inquire about Vimalakirti's illness. But each in turn declines to do so, relating an incident in the past when he was reproved by Vimalakirti for some fault in his understanding or practice of the doctrine. The Buddha then asks various outstanding bodhisattvas to carry out his request, but they too express reluctance to do so for similar reasons. Finally the bodhisattva Manjushri, who in Buddhist lore symbolizes the perfection of wisdom, agrees to carry out the Buddha's request. Countless members of the assembly, eager to witness the encounter between these two renowned figures, Manjushri and Vimalakirti, accompany Manjushri on his mission.

The scene then shifts to Vimalakirti's sickroom, a narrow cell that nevertheless is miraculously able to accommodate the vast throngs who have come to visit him. In the chapters that follow, Vimalakirti, Manjushri, and other members of the group are shown engaging in discussions of the Dharma or Buddhist truth.

In chapter 11 the scene shifts back to the Amra Gardens, where Vimalakirti and Manjushri join Shakyamuni Buddha for further expositions of the doctrine and various astonishing demonstrations of their supernatural powers. The work concludes with conventional praises of the sutra itself and an "entrustment" scene in which Shakyamuni calls on the bodhisattva Maitreya, who is destined to be the next Buddha to appear in this world, to guard the sutra and insure that it is widely propagated.

## Early Buddhism

In order to fully understand the events narrated in the sutra, particularly those relating to the monk-disciples of the Buddha, we must briefly survey the early history of the Buddhist religion.

Shakyamuni Buddha, the founder of Buddhism, who is also known by the name *Gautama*, appears to have lived in India sometime around the sixth or fifth century B.C.E. Though it is

3

difficult to describe his doctrines in detail, Buddhologists customarily accept several formulas as representative of his teachings. Most famous of these are the so-called four noble truths, which are referred to in several places in the Vimalakirti Sutra. These teach that (1) all existence in the saha world,[1] the world in which we live at present, is marked by suffering; (2) that suffering is caused by craving or desire; (3) that by doing away with craving one can gain release from suffering and reach a state of peace and enlightenment known as nirvana or tranquil extinction; (4) that there is a method for achieving this goal, namely, the discipline known as the eightfold path. This is a set of moral principles enjoining one to cultivate right views, right thinking, right speech, right action, right way of life, right endeavor, right mindfulness, and right meditation.

Another doctrine, also referred to in the Vimalakirti Sutra and at one point negated by it, is that of the twelve-linked chain of causation or dependent origination, which step by step illustrates the causal relationship between ignorance and suffering. The purpose of the doctrine, like that of the four noble truths, is to wake one to the true nature of reality and help one to achieve emancipation from ignorance and suffering.

Buddhism took over from earlier Indian thought the concept of karma, the belief that the deeds done in present or past existences will determine the circumstances into which one will be reborn in the future. According to the Indian view, living beings pass through an endless cycle of death and rebirth, and the ill effects of an evil action in one lifetime may not become evident until some later existence; but that they will appear eventually is inescapable.

The Buddha's eightfold path, as we have seen, offers a prescription for freeing oneself from ignorance and evil, advancing

4

---

1. See the glossary for further information on the saha world and other technical terms used in the introduction and translation.

one's level of spiritual attainment, and perhaps even escaping the cycle of birth and death entirely. But in order to pursue that path with appropriate zeal and concentration, it was thought all but imperative that one leave secular or household life and become a member of the Buddhist order, which consisted of both monks and nuns. There, free from family entanglements and mundane concerns, one could devote oneself to a life of poverty, celibacy, and religious study and discipline, supported by the alms of the lay community. Lay believers could acquire religious merit by assisting the order, observing appropriate rules of moral conduct, and carrying out devotional practices. But it was thought that they would have to wait until some future existence, when they too could become members of the order, before they could hope to gain full release from the bonds of suffering.

In early Buddhism, the ultimate goal of religious striving was to reach the state of arhat, a "worthy" or "saint," one who has overcome desire; passed beyond samsara, the world of suffering and cyclical birth and death; and entered nirvana. But as the monastic community labored in the centuries following the Buddha's demise to systematize his teachings and clarify points upon which, perhaps intentionally, his pronouncements had been vague, a number of doctrinal problems arose. Just what were the characteristics of an arhat, of a Buddha, or of the state of nirvana? What is the exact nature of the dharmas, the myriad objects and phenomena that make up the world as we know it through the senses? If, as the Buddha taught, there is no such thing as an individual self or ego, then what is it that is the recipient of karmic retribution? The members of the order, in their efforts to settle questions such as these, became increasingly occupied with codification of the tenets and doctrinal issues, and the religious body split up into a number of sects or schools that differed in matters of interpretation and practice.

These tenets and practices of early Buddhism that I have been describing are often referred to as Hinayana or the "Lesser

5

Vehicle," a derogatory term applied to them by a rival group within the religion that labeled itself Mahayana or the "Great Vehicle" and represented its doctrines as superior to and superseding those of earlier Buddhism. The Mahayana movement appears to have begun in India around the first or second century of the Common Era. In part it was probably a reaction against the great emphasis upon monastic life that marked earlier Buddhism and against the arid psychological and metaphysical speculations that characterize much of early Buddhist scholasticism. It sought to open up the religious life to a wider proportion of the population, to accord a more important role to lay believers, and to give more appealing expression to the teachings and make them more readily accessible.

In earlier Buddhism, as I have already noted, the aim of religious practice was to achieve the state of arhat, one who has gained release from suffering and passed beyond the confines of this world. But to the members of the Mahayana movement this seemed too selfish an objective, one that was too at variance with the spirit of compassion and concern for all living beings that they regarded as the soul of Buddhist teachings.

In contrast to the state of arhat, they chose as their goal and ideal the figure of the bodhisattva, one who vows not only to achieve enlightenment for himself but to assist all others to do likewise. He advances stage by stage in his spiritual progress until he has reached the point where he could, if he wished, enter nirvana. But he—or she, since Mahayana largely disregards distinctions of gender—out of motives of compassion deliberately elects to remain in the realm of birth and death, permitting himself to be reborn as a human being, an animal, or even a dweller in hell in order to assist others and guide them on the path to salvation. It is this spirit of altruism that most of all distinguishes the bodhisattva from the follower of Hinayana teachings.

Earlier Buddhism often described Shakyamuni Buddha as a bodhisattva in his previous existences, when he was still advancing toward enlightenment. But in Mahayana texts such as the Vimalakirti Sutra the bodhisattvas are depicted as limitless in number, all-seeing and all-caring, capable of extending unbounded aid to others in the search for enlightenment. Indeed, this great emphasis on the role of the bodhisattva is one of the main characteristics that distinguishes Mahayana thought from that of earlier Buddhism, and much of the present work is devoted to descriptions of the bodhisattva ideal.

Vimalakirti himself, as revealed in chapter 12 of the Vimalakirti Sutra, in his previous existence had been a bodhisattva in the realm of a Buddha named Akshobhya or Immovable. But he abandoned that land of purity and deliberately chose to be reborn in our present saha world in the time of Shakyamuni Buddha so that he could assist in expounding the Law of the Buddhas. He speaks from a level of wisdom and authority equal to that of the Buddhas themselves, and his expositions are aimed at expounding the ideals of Mahayana Buddhism and refuting the views and practices of the Hinayana followers.

These latter are represented in the sutra in particular by Shakyamuni's ten major disciples, who are referred to as voice-hearers. The term originally designated persons in Shakyamuni's lifetime who had entered the monastic order and had heard the teachings directly from him, though later it came to refer to those monks and nuns who adhered to Hinayana beliefs and strove to attain the state of arhat.

A second and less important target of Vimalakirti's criticism is the pratyekabuddhas, "private Buddhas" or "self-enlightened ones," beings who have won an understanding of the truth through their own efforts but who make no attempt to teach others or assist them to enlightenment. These two groups, the voice-hearers and the pratyekabuddhas, are the frequent objects of Vimalakirti's reproaches, and at times even ridicule, because of their limited and self-centered aims and procedures, as contrasted with those of the bodhisattvas.

The sutra as a whole, then, represents both a critique of earlier Buddhist doctrines and an exposition, as vivid and compelling as the author or authors could make it, of those of the newly risen Mahayana movement. They did not hesitate to set the scene of their exposition back in time, in the era of Shakyamuni Buddha, no doubt because in the fervor of their faith they were convinced that they were conveying to the world the true meaning of Shakyamuni's message.

Though the sutra ostensibly depicts events taking place in Shakyamuni's lifetime, it makes no pretense at conforming to historical reality, or even to conventional concepts of time and space. According to the Mahayana conception of the universe, the world we live in at present is made up of four continents ranged around a great central mountain, Mount Sumeru. We live in the continent located to the south, known as Jambudvipa or the "continent of the *jambu* trees." Underneath it are various hells where beings who have committed particularly evil deeds must suffer for a time, and above it a series of heavens occupied by the gods who, though happier than human beings, are bound like them to the cycle of birth and death.

Outside of our present world there exist countless others spread out in all directions, some similarly made up of four continents, others fabulous realms presided over by various Buddhas, for in the Mahayana teachings, Buddhas as well as bodhisattvas have become infinite in number. Through their supernatural powers, the Buddhas, bodhisattvas, and guardian deities such as the Brahmas, Indras, and Four Heavenly Kings of these various worlds can travel at will from one world to another. Thus in the opening chapter of the Vimalakirti Sutra we find Shakyamuni addressing a staggering multitude of listeners that includes Brahmas and Indras who have come from other worlds to listen to his message, as well as various nonhuman beings such as dragons, garuda birds, and other figures drawn from Indian mythology. The Mahayana version of the

Dharma, we are to understand, is addressed not to humans alone but to all beings whatsoever. The events depicted in the sutra represent a mixture of realistic scenes from early Indian life—the Buddha's monk disciples begging for alms in a nearby village, practicing meditation in the forest, or fetching fresh milk for the Buddha when he is indisposed—and a bizarre assortment of *Alice in Wonderland*-like personages and happenings that display the Mahayana imagination at its most fertile. These include a mischievous goddess, invisible at most times, who inhabits Vimalakirti's room and has overheard and profited from his teachings, a phantom bodhisattva who journeys to a realm "beyond Buddha lands numerous as the sands of forty-two Ganges" to beg for leftover food, five hundred little parasols that are combined to form one parasol so big it can spread over the entire universe, or thirty-two thousand large chairs somehow fitted into Vimalakirti's tiny sickroom. This juxtaposition of mundane and fantastic elements is meant to point up the contrast between the earnest but circumscribed goals and ways of thought characteristic of the Hinayana school, and the incomparably freer and loftier ones of the Mahayana. To understand the contrast, and the Mahayana claims to superiority that it represents, we must turn now to the doctrine of emptiness on which such claims rest.

9

## The Doctrine of Nondualism

Vimalakirti's criticisms of Hinayana and his own expositions of the Dharma center around the concept of emptiness or nondualism, a key tenet in Mahayana thought. Like so much in Mahayana, it represents an extension and elaboration of ideas already present in early Buddhism. The Buddha had taught that all things in the phenomenal world are conditioned in nature, brought into being and governed by causes and conditions. They are thus in a state of constant flux and are destined to change and pass away. They may therefore be designated as "empty" or "void" because they lack any inherent characteristics by which they can be described, changing as they do from instant to instant. At best they can be delineated by what they are not—not permanent, not possessed of any fixed form or self-nature.

The formulators of Mahayana doctrine, while taking over these ideas, preferred to emphasize not the negative but rather the positive aspects or import of this concept of emptiness. If all phenomena are characterized by the quality of emptiness, then emptiness must constitute the unchanging and abiding nature of existence. Seen from the point of view of differentiation, things fall into numberless different categories. But looked at from the point of view of emptiness, they are seen to have one quality they all share: that of forming a single entity, one that is beyond the power of language to describe because language can deal only with distinctions, a point that Vimalakirti dramatically emphasizes at the end of chapter 9.

To help the reader visualize the concept more clearly, I would like here to offer an analogy. Experts may object that my analogy is theoretically unsound. But that could probably be said of any analogy that attempts to convey in words a truth that is beyond verbal expression, so I will venture it anyway.

Let the reader imagine a round paper fan. One face of the fan is covered with an infinite number of tiny dots representing all the multiple objects and ideas that make up our ordinary world, the endless dualisms of here/there, now/then, big/little, beautiful/ugly that confront us daily, dots that are continually shifting, appearing and disappearing in an unending cycle of change. This is the phenomenal world, brought into being, says the Buddha, by causes and conditions, undergoing a ceaseless process of arising and cessation, the world of samsara or cyclical birth and death.

But now turn the fan over. The other face is a complete blank, every trace of differentiation obliterated. This is the world of emptiness, of nondualism, the transcendent realm as opposed to the imminent. The two worlds are one: everything that was present on the other face of the fan is encompassed within the blank one, but everything has become "equal" or fused with everything else, because everything is identical with emptiness. "Form is emptiness, emptiness is form," says the Heart Sutra, a statement that is found in the Vimalakirti Sutra as well, and the same equation applies to perception, conception, volition, and consciousness, the other terms that make up the five aggregates or components of existence in the phenomenal world.

In this world of emptiness, the dimensions of space and time no longer exist, since all distinctions between here and there, now or never have been wiped out. Nothing comes into existence or passes into extinction, because there is no other place to come from or go to, because terms such as being or nonbeing have no meaning here. Because of its underlying unity, all things in it interpenetrate with one another and share one another's identity, which leads the Mahayana proponents to assert that all beings partake of the Buddha nature and hence have the potential to attain Buddhahood. And the same reasoning leads them to proclaim that earthly desires are none other than bodhi or the state of enlightenment, and that samsara, the ordinary world of suffering, is none other than nirvana.

Vimalakirti, in his expositions of the Dharma and particularly when he is addressing the voice-hearers or representatives of Hinayana thought, lays great emphasis upon the doctrine of emptiness, deliberately employing expressions that he knows will seem paradoxical or shocking to them. It is his method of jarring them, and readers as well, out of their habitual modes of thinking.

But Buddhism in all things stresses moderation or the Middle Way, the path that lies between two extremes. Because the followers of Hinayana seem too engrossed with distinctions between pure and impure, common mortal and enlightened being, the monastic community and the laity, Vimalakirti calls their attention to the realm of nondualism where all such distinctions are transcended. But he is not asking them to abandon all distinctions unconditionally. What he is calling for is an outlook that will somehow balance or hold in suspension the two seemingly contradictory views of reality and prevent either from becoming unduly dominant.

As frequently pointed out, the concept of emptiness or nondualism, if carried to its logical extreme, will effectively wipe out the foundations upon which the religion rests. One can hardly urge people to observe difficult precepts or codes of moral behavior while assuring them that in the end there is no difference between right and wrong, or expect them to strive to attain religious goals that one has declared to be nonexistent. And simply as a matter of common sense, it is obvious that one cannot hope to carry out daily activities on the basis of nondualistic principles alone. No pedestrian in a modern city, for example, who thinks that red lights and green lights are all one and the same will survive for long. But the nondualistic outlook can be used to leaven and enlarge our everyday ways of thinking, to warn us away from excessive emotional involvement in our undertakings, from excessive pride in our achievements, or to help us resign ourselves to ills that are beyond our control.

The doctrine of nondualism is not intended to be an objective description of the true nature of reality, but rather a recommendation as to how one can best view reality in order to advance one's religious aims, a tool to assist one in realizing the Middle Way. Like all doctrines in Mahayana, it is provisional in nature, and to cling to it too tenaciously would be as reprehensible as any other form of clinging or attachment. Yet without it, one cannot hope to view the everyday world in its proper perspective.

In Mahayana Buddhism, one does not "grasp" or acquire anything new when one attains enlightenment, since according to Mahayana belief all beings have from the beginning been endowed with the Buddha nature. One does not migrate to some new realm or life condition, but simply comes to realize the true nature of the realm one is in. As the Vimalakirti Sutra states in one of its most famous pronouncements: "When the mind is pure, the Buddha land will be pure." And it is the doctrine of nondualism that guides one to this understanding.

This doctrine, seeming as it does to contradict all the assumptions of our everyday modes of thought, is not easy to visualize, however, and there will perhaps be things about the figure of Vimalakirti and about his teachings that, initially at least, puzzle the reader. His pronouncements, though deliberately couched in paradoxical language, appear logical enough if we consider them in the light of nondualism. And the exhilarating freedom from limitations of time and space experienced by one who has broken through into this realm of emptiness or the absolute are given striking symbolic expression in the sutra by the various miracles or displays of supernatural powers performed by Vimalakirti or the Buddhas. But the reader might well wish to know more precisely just how one goes about practicing the six paramitas or "perfections"—almsgiving, keeping of the precepts, forbearance, assiduousness, meditation, and wisdom—a prime requirement for bodhisattvas, while holding fast to the doctrine of nondualism. Or, to put it in more specific terms, to learn how Vimalakirti manages to combine true Buddhist wisdom and detachment with the life of the layman, how he can head a family, conduct business affairs, and fulfill his other obligations as a citizen of the city of Vaishali and still remain faithful to the bodhisattva ideal.

The Vimalakirti Sutra, however, seems to delight more in confronting us with contradictions and dilemmas than in offering easy answers. It is a deliberately challenging text, one that utilizes all the drama, wit, humor, and persuasiveness of lan-

13

guage it can summon up in order to waken us to new dimensions of thought, new levels of religious understanding and action of which we had previously been unaware. In doing so, it vividly reflects the spirit of the Mahayana movement in one of its most creative and inspired moments.

*The Vimalakirti Sutra*

*Chapter 1*

This is what I heard:

At one time the Buddha was in the Amra Gardens in the city of Vaishali, accompanied by a multitude of leading monks numbering eight thousand. There were also thirty-two thousand bodhisattvas, all known to the assembly, persons who had carried out all the basic practices of great wisdom. Sustained by the might and supernatural powers of the Buddhas, they accepted and upheld the correct Law in order to guard the citadel of the Dharma. They knew how to roar the lion's roar, and their fame resounded in the ten directions. Without waiting to be asked, they befriended others and brought them comfort. They ensured the continuance and prosperity of the Three Treasures, making certain that these never expired. They conquered and subdued the ill will of the devils and curbed the non-Buddhist doctrines.

All were spotless and pure, having long ago rid themselves of snares and obstructions; their minds constantly resided in a state of unhindered emancipation. Their mindfulness, meditation, retention of the teachings, and eloquence never faltered, and of almsgiving, keeping of the precepts, forbearance, assiduousness, meditation, wisdom, and the power to employ expedient means, there was not one they were deficient in.

They had learned to accept the fact that there is nothing to be grasped at, no view of phenomena to be entertained. They knew how to respond compliantly to others and to turn the unregressing wheel of the Law. Expert in comprehending the characteristics of phenomena, able to understand the capacities of living beings, they towered over the others of the great assembly and had learned to be fearful of nothing.

With their merits and wisdom they disciplined their minds; they adorned their bodies with auspicious signs, ranking foremost in aspect and form, but rejected all worldly embellishments. In fame and renown they soared higher than Mount Sumeru; their profound faith was diamondlike in its firmness. The jewels of their Dharma shone everywhere, raining down sweet dew, and among the assembly the sound of their words was the most subtle and wonderful of all.

They had plumbed the depths of dependent origination and cut off all erroneous views, no longer entertaining the concepts either of being or nonbeing. In expounding the Law they were fearless as roaring lions, and their disquisitions on it rolled forth like thunder. There was no measuring them, for they had passed beyond measure. In seeking out the jewels of the Dharma, they were like practiced pilots at sea. They had mastered all the profound and subtle meanings of the doctrines and were expert in perceiving the past and future existences of living beings and the workings of their minds.

They came close to equaling the freely exercised wisdom of the Buddha, the unparalleled one, his ten powers, his fearlessness, and his eighteen unshared properties. Though they had firmly closed the gate to all manner of evil existences, yet they allowed themselves to be born in the five lower realms, manifesting themselves there so that they might act as great physician kings, adroitly healing the ills of others, doling out whatever medicine suited the ailment, and insuring that the patient took it as prescribed.

Countless benefits—all these they had acquired; countless Buddha lands—all these they had made marvelously pure. No one saw or listened to them without profiting thereby, and no action of theirs was ever performed in vain. Such was the manner in which all merits adhered to them.

The names of the bodhisattvas were Bodhisattva Viewing Equality, Bodhisattva Viewing Inequality, Bodhisattva Viewing

Equality and Inequality, Bodhisattva Meditation Freedom King, Bodhisattva Dharma Freedom King, Bodhisattva Dharma Forms, Bodhisattva Shining Forms, Bodhisattva Shining Adornment, Bodhisattva Great Adornment, Bodhisattva Jeweled Accumulation, Bodhisattva Accumulation of Eloquence, Bodhisattva Jeweled Hand, Bodhisattva Jeweled Seal Hand, Bodhisattva Constantly Raised Hand, Bodhisattva Constantly Extended Hand, Bodhisattva Constantly Commiserating, Bodhisattva Joyful Capacity, Bodhisattva Joyful King, Bodhisattva Eloquent Sound, Bodhisattva Storehouse of Emptiness, Bodhisattva Holder of the Jeweled Torch, Bodhisattva Jeweled Valor, Bodhisattva Jeweled View, Bodhisattva of Indra's Net, Bodhisattva Bright Net, Bodhisattva Unconditioned View, Bodhisattva Wisdom Accumulation, Bodhisattva Jeweled Supremacy, Bodhisattva Heavenly King, Bodhisattva Devil Defeating, Bodhisattva Lightning Virtue, Bodhisattva Freedom King, Bodhisattva Merit Forms and Adornments, Bodhisattva Lion's Roar, Bodhisattva Thunder Sound, Bodhisattva Mountain Form Smiting Sound, Bodhisattva Rutting Elephant, Bodhisattva White Rutting Elephant, Bodhisattva Constant Exertion, Bodhisattva Never Resting, Bodhisattva Wonderful Birth, Bodhisattva Flower Adornment, Bodhisattva Perceiver of the World's Sounds, Bodhisattva Gainer of Great Authority, Bodhisattva of Brahma's Net, Bodhisattva Jeweled Staff, Bodhisattva Unsurpassed, Bodhisattva Adorned Land, Bodhisattva Golden Locks, Bodhisattva Gemmed Locks, Bodhisattva Maitreya, and Bodhisattva Dharma Prince Manjushri. There were thirty-two thousand bodhisattvas such as these

There were also ten thousand Brahma kings, Shikhin and others, who had come from the other four-continent worlds to visit the place where the Buddha was and listen to the Dharma. There were also twelve thousand Indras who had come from the other four-continent worlds to take a seat in the gathering. In addition, there were other heavenly beings of great authority and power, as well as dragons, spirits, yakshas, gandharvas, asuras, garudas, kimnaras, mahoragas, and others, all come to take a seat in the assembly. Also arrived to take seats in the assembly were the various monks, nuns, laymen, and laywomen.

At that time the Buddha, reverently surrounded by this multitude of countless hundreds and thousands of beings, expounded the Law for them. He was like Mount Sumeru, king of mountains, rising up out of the great sea. Resting at ease in his lion's seat clustered with jewels, he shed his radiance over all the great throng gathered there.

At that time a man named Jeweled Accumulation, son of a wealthy man of the city of Vaishali, along with five hundred other sons of wealthy men, had come to the place where the Buddha was, all of them bearing parasols adorned with the seven treasures. Bowing their heads in obeisance before the feet of the Buddha, they joined in offering their parasols as alms to the Buddha.

The Buddha with his supernatural powers then caused all the jeweled parasols to come together and form one single parasol that spread over the entire thousand-millionfold world. All the vast features of that world were visible there in its midst. All the Mount Sumerus of the thousand-millionfold world, Snow Mountains, Muchilinda Mountains, Mahamuchilinda Mountains, Fragrant Mountains, Jeweled Mountains, Gold Mountains, Black Mountains, Iron Encircling Mountains, Great Iron Encircling Mountains, the huge seas, the rivers and watercourses, brooks and streams, fountains and springs, as well as the suns, moons, stars, constellations, heavenly palaces, dragon palaces, and the palaces of the venerable spirits—all these were to be seen within the jeweled parasol. And the Buddhas of the ten directions, the Buddhas as they preached the Law—these too were visible within the jeweled parasol.

At that time all the members of the great assembly, witnessing this manifestation of the Buddha's supernatural powers, sighed in admiration at what they had never seen before. Pressing their palms together, they made obeisance to the Buddha, gazing up in reverence at the face of the Honored One and never taking their eyes from it.

Then the rich man's son, Jeweled Accumulation, in the presence of the Buddha recited these verses of praise:

> Eyes pure and broad like the blue lotus;
> mind pure, steeped in meditations;
> for pure deeds long accumulated, boundless
>     in fame,
> your quietude guides the assembly—thus we
>     bow our heads.
>
> We have seen the great sage work miraculous
>     transformations,
> showing us all the countless lands in ten
>     directions,
> the Buddhas expounding the Law therein—
> every one of these we have seen and heard.
>
> The Dharma King's Dharma powers surpass
>     all other beings,
> constantly he bestows Dharma riches on
>     them all.
> Skillfully he distinguishes the characteristics
>     of phenomena,
> never faltering in his grasp of the one great
>     Truth.
>
> You have learned to treat all phenomena with
>     freedom,
> so we bow our heads to this Dharma King.
> You define things as neither existing nor not

21

existing;
causes and conditions bring about their birth.

No "I," no doer, no recipient,
yet good and bad karma never cease to
      function.
Beneath the Buddha tree, you used your
      might to overpower the devil;
gaining the sweet dew of nirvana, you won
      your way to enlightenment.

Already free of thought, perception, and
      volition,
you refuted all the non-Buddhist doctrines.
Three times you turned the wheel of the Law
      in the thousand-millionfold world,
the wheel that from the first has always
      been pure.

Heavenly and human beings gained the
      way—this was proof of it;
the Three Treasures thereupon appeared in
      the world.
This wonderful Law brought rescue to the
      many beings;
embracing it, they never regress but dwell in
      constant quietude.

Great physician king, healer of old age, sick-
      ness and death,
we pay homage to the boundless virtue of
      your Dharma sea;
unmoved by acclamation or abuse, like
      Mount Sumeru,

you pity in equal measure the good and the
    not good.

In mind and action impartial, like the empty
    sky—
who can hark to this jewel of humankind, not
    give respectful assent?
Now we offer these little parasols to the
    World-Honored One,
and in them is revealed to us the three thou-
    sand worlds.

Palaces where gods, dragons, and spirits
    reside,
kimnaras, yakshas, and all those other beings,
everything that exists in the world we see—
the ten-powered one in pity manifests these
    transformations.

The assembly, seeing this rare sight, all praise
    the Buddha;
now we bow our heads to the venerable one of
    the threefold world.
Great sage, Dharma King, refuge of the multi-
    tude—
viewing the Buddha with purified mind, none
    who do not rejoice!

Each sees the World-Honored One standing
    right before him—
such are the Buddha's transcendental powers,
    his unshared properties.
The Buddha preaches the Law with a single
    voice,

but each living being understands it according
    to his kind.

All believe the World-Honored One speaks
    the same words to all—
such are his transcendental powers, his
    unshared properties.
The Buddha preaches the Law with a single
    voice,
but each living being understands it in his
    own way.

All undertake the Buddha's practices and gain
    profit thereby—
such are his transcendental powers, his
    unshared properties.
The Buddha preaches the Law with a single
    voice,
but to some it brings fear, to others delight
    and joy.

Some are moved to leave the world, some are
    freed of doubt—
such are his transcendental powers, his
    unshared properties.
Before the great diligence of the ten-powered
    one we bow our heads;
we bow our heads to the fearlessness he has
    attained.

We bow heads before the one who dwells in
    unshared properties,
bow heads before the great leader of all beings.
You can cut the thongs that bind the multi-
    tude—we bow heads to that;

you crossed to the other shore—we bow
　　heads to that.

We bow heads to one who can save all those
　　in this world,
bow heads to one who long ago left the path
　　of birth and death.
You know the marks of all beings in their
　　comings and goings,
you have gained apt liberation from all
　　phenomena.

Free of worldly attachments, like the lotus
　　blossom,
constantly you move within the realm of
　　emptiness and quiet;
you have mastered the marks of all phenom-
　　ena, no blocks or hindrances;
like the sky, you lean on nothing—we bow
　　our heads!

When the rich man's son, Jeweled Accumulation, had finished reciting these verses, he addressed the Buddha, saying,
"World-Honored One, these five hundred sons of rich men
have all set their minds on anuttara-samyak-sambodhi. They
wish to hear how one can purify the Buddha lands.[1] We beg the
World-Honored One to explain the practices carried out by
bodhisattvas in purifying the lands."

The Buddha said, "Excellent, Jeweled Accumulation! For the
sake of the bodhisattvas you do right to ask the Thus Come
One about the practices for purifying the lands. Listen well,

25

1. To "purify the Buddha lands" here means to work diligently to lead the
　beings of various realms or Buddha lands to enlightenment, which is one
　of the chief aims of the bodhisattva's activities.

listen well, and mull it over in your thoughts! I will now explain to you."

Jeweled Accumulation and the other five hundred sons of rich men then made ready to listen to the teachings addressed to them.

The Buddha said, "Jeweled Accumulation, the various kinds of living beings are in themselves the Buddha lands of the bodhisattvas. Why so? Because it is by converting various beings to the teachings that the bodhisattvas acquire their Buddha lands. It is by persuading various beings and overcoming their objections that the bodhisattvas acquire their Buddha lands. It is by inducing the various living beings to enter into the Buddha wisdom in such-and-such a land that they acquire their Buddha lands. It is by inducing the various living beings to develop the capacity for bodhisattva practices in such-and-such a land that they acquire their Buddha lands.

"Why is this? Because the bodhisattva's acquisition of a pure land is wholly due to his having brought benefit to living beings. Suppose a man proposes to build a mansion on a plot of open land. He may do so as he wishes without hindrance. But if he tries to build it in the empty air, he will never be successful. It is the same with the bodhisattvas. It is because they wish to help others to achieve success that they take their vow to acquire Buddha lands. Their vow to acquire Buddha lands in not founded on emptiness.

"Jeweled Accumulation, you should understand that an upright mind is the pure land of the bodhisattva.[2] When the

2. *The term* chih-hsin, *"upright mind," may also be translated "straightforward mind" or "direct mind." In the paragraphs that follow, the term "pure land" is being used to mean a state of mind or course of action that allows a bodhisattva to create a Buddha land that is pure in nature by leading others to enlightenment. The quality or action in the bodhisattva produces a similar state in the beings who are born in his land; for example, because he himself is honest and upright in mind, they are free from flattery or deviousness.*

bodhisattva attains Buddhahood, then beings who are free of flattery will be born in his country.

"A deeply searching mind is the pure land of the bodhisattva. When he attains Buddhahood, beings who are endowed with blessings will be born in his country.

"A mind that aspires to bodhi or enlightenment is the pure land of the bodhisattva. When he attains Buddhahood, beings dedicated to the Great Vehicle will be born in his country.

"Almsgiving is the pure land of the bodhisattva. When he attains Buddhahood, beings who are capable of casting away everything will be born in his country.

"Keeping of the precepts is the pure land of the bodhisattva. When he attains Buddhahood, beings who fulfill their vow to carry out the ten good actions will be born in his country.

"Forbearance is the pure land of the bodhisattva. When he attains Buddhahood, beings who are adorned with the thirty-two features will be born in his country.

"Assiduousness is the pure land of the bodhisattva. When he attains Buddhahood, beings who strive diligently to acquire all manner of blessings will be born in his country.

"Meditation is the pure land of the bodhisattva. When he attains Buddhahood, beings who can regulate their minds and keep them from disorder will be born in his country.

"Wisdom is the pure land of the bodhisattva. When he attains Buddhahood, beings who are correct and certain in understanding will be born in his country.

"A mind devoted to the four immeasurable qualities is the pure land of the bodhisattva. When he attains Buddhahood, beings perfect in the exercise of pity, compassion, joy, and indifference will be born in his country.

"The four methods of winning people are the pure land of the bodhisattva. When he attains Buddhahood, beings who are regulated by the emancipations will be born in his country.

"Expedient means are the pure land of the bodhisattva. When he attains Buddhahood, beings who can employ all manner of expedient means with complete freedom will be born in his country.

"The thirty-seven elements of the Way are the pure land of the bodhisattva. When he attains Buddhahood, beings will be born in his country who are proficient in the four states of mindfulness, the four types of correct effort, the four bases of supernatural power, the five roots of goodness, the five powers, the seven factors of enlightenment, and the eightfold holy path.

"A mind intent on transferring merit to others is the pure land of the bodhisattva. When he attains Buddhahood, he will acquire a country endowed with all manner of blessings.

"Teaching others to avoid the eight difficulties is the pure land of the bodhisattva. When he attains Buddhahood, his country will be free of the three evils and the eight difficulties.

"Observing the precepts himself but not taxing others with their shortcomings is the pure land of the bodhisattva. When he attains Buddhahood, no one in his country will be called a violator of prohibitions.

"The ten good actions are the pure land of the bodhisattva. When he attains Buddhahood, beings will be born in his country who suffer no untimely death, possess great wealth, are pure in action, sincere and truthful in word, ever mild in speech, never alienated from kin or associates, skillful in solving disputes, invariably speaking profitable words, never envious, never irate, and correct in understanding.[3]

"Therefore, Jeweled Accumulation, because the bodhisattva has an upright mind, he is impelled to action. Because he is impelled to action, he gains a deeply searching mind. Because he has a deeply searching mind, his will is well controlled. Because his will is well controlled, he acts in accord with the teachings. Because he acts in accord with the teachings, he can transfer

28

3. *Each of the ten merits listed here results from the observance of one of the ten good actions.*

merit to others. Because he transfers merit to others, he knows how to employ expedient means. Because he knows how to employ expedient means, he can lead others to enlightenment. Because he leads others to enlightenment, his Buddha land is pure. Because his Buddha land is pure, his preaching of the Law is pure. Because his preaching of the Law is pure, his wisdom is pure. Because his wisdom is pure, his mind is pure. And because his mind is pure, all the blessings he enjoys will be pure.

"Therefore, Jeweled Accumulation, if the bodhisattva wishes to acquire a pure land, he must purify his mind. When the mind is pure, the Buddha land will be pure."

At that time Shariputra, moved by the Buddha's supernatural powers, thought to himself: "If the mind of the bodhisattva is pure, then his Buddha land will be pure. Now when our World-Honored One first determined to become a bodhisattva, surely his intentions were pure. Why then is this Buddha land so filled with impurities?"[4]

The Buddha, knowing his thoughts, said to him, "What do you think? Are the sun and moon impure? Is that why the blind man fails to see them?"

Shariputra replied, "No, World-Honored One. That is the fault of the blind man. The sun and moon are not to blame."

"Shariputra, it is the failings of living beings that prevent them from seeing the marvelous purity of the land of the Buddha, the Thus Come One. The Thus Come One is not to blame. Shariputra, this land of mine is pure, but you fail to see it."

At that time one of the Brahma kings with his conch-shaped tuft of hair said to Shariputra, "You must not think that this

4. *Shariputra, one of the Buddha's ten major disciples, customarily appears in the Vimalakirti Sutra as an expresser of doubts or expounder of erroneous views associated with Hinayana teachings. But as indicated here, the Buddha at times deliberately implants such doubts in Shariputra's mind as a means of furthering the exposition of the doctrine.*

Buddha land is impure. Why do I say this? Because to my eyes, Shakyamuni's Buddha land is as pure and spotless as the palace of the heavenly being Great Freedom."

Shariputra said, "When I look at this land, I see it full of knolls and hollows, thorny underbrush, sand and gravel, dirt, rocks, many mountains, filth and defilement."

The Brahma king said, "It is just that your mind has highs and lows and does not rest on Buddha wisdom. Therefore you see this land as impure. Shariputra, the bodhisattva treats all things and beings, each one of them, with perfect equality. His deeply searching mind is pure, and because it rests on Buddha wisdom, it can see the purity of this Buddha land."

The Buddha then pressed his toe against the earth, and immediately the thousand-millionfold world was adorned with hundreds and thousands of rare jewels, till it resembled Jeweled Adornment Buddha's Jeweled Adornment Land of Immeasurable Blessings. All the members of the great assembly sighed in wonder at what they had never seen before, and all saw that they themselves were seated on jeweled lotuses.[5]

The Buddha said to Shariputra, "Now do you see the marvelous purity of this Buddha land?"

Shariputra replied, "Indeed I do, World-Honored One. Something I have never seen before, and never even heard of—now all the marvelous purity of the Buddha land is visible before me!"

The Buddha said to Shariputra, "My Buddha land has always been pure like this. But because I wish to save those persons who are lowly and inferior, I make it seem an impure land full of defilements, that is all. It is like the case of heavenly beings. All take their food from the same precious vessel, but the food looks different for each one, depending upon the merits and virtues that each possesses. It is the same in this case, Shariputra. If a

---

5. *That is, they perceived that they themselves were possessed of the Buddha nature.*

person's mind is pure, then he will see the wonderful blessings that adorn this land."

When the Buddha in this way revealed the marvelous purity of the land, the five hundred sons of rich men who accompanied Jeweled Accumulation all were able to grasp the truth of birthlessness, and eighty-four thousand persons all set their minds on attaining anuttara-samyak-sambodhi. The Buddha then released the supernatural power that he had exercised with his toe and the world returned to its former appearance.

Thirty-two thousand heavenly and human beings who wished to pursue the path of the voice-hearer, understanding that all things are impermanent in nature, cast off the dust, removed themselves from defilement, and attained the pure Dharma eye; and eight thousand monks, ceasing to accept the phenomenal world, put an end to all outflows and gained emancipation of mind.

## Chapter 2

EXPEDIENT MEANS

At that time in the great city of Vaishali there was a rich man named Vimalakirti. Already in the past he had offered alms to immeasurable numbers of Buddhas, had deeply planted the roots of goodness, and had grasped the truth of birthlessness. Unhindered in his eloquence, able to disport himself with transcendental powers, he commanded full retention of the teachings and had attained the state of fearlessness. He had overcome the torments and ill will of the devil and entered deeply into the doctrine of the Law, proficient in the paramita of wisdom and a master in the employing of expedient means. He had successfully fulfilled his great vow and could clearly discern how the minds of others were tending. Moreover, he could distinguish whether their capacities were keen or obtuse. His mind was cleansed and purified through long practice of the Buddha Way, firm in its grasp of the Great Vehicle, and all his actions were well thought out and planned. He maintained the dignity and authority of a Buddha, and his mind was vast as the sea. All the Buddhas sighed with admiration, and he commanded the respect of the disciples, of Indra, Brahma, and the Four Heavenly Kings.

Desiring to save others, he employed the excellent expedient of residing in Vaishali. His immeasurable riches he used to relieve the poor, his faultless observation of the precepts served as a reproach to those who would violate prohibitions. Through his restraint and forbearance he warned others against rage and anger, and his great assiduousness discouraged all thought of sloth and indolence. Concentrating his single mind in quiet meditation, he suppressed disordered

32

thoughts; through firm and unwavering wisdom he overcame all that was not wise.[1]

Though dressed in the white robes of a layman, he observed all the rules of pure conduct laid down for monks, and though he lived at home, he felt no attachment to the threefold world. One could see he had a wife and children, yet he was at all times chaste in action; obviously he had kin and household attendants, yet he always delighted in withdrawing from them. Although he wore jewels and finery, his real adornment was the auspicious marks; although he ate and drank like others, what he truly savored was the joy of meditation.

If he visited the gambling parlors, it was solely to bring enlightenment to those there; if he listened to the doctrines of other religions, he did not allow them to impinge on the true faith. Though well versed in secular writings, his constant delight was in the Buddhist Law. Respected by everyone, he was looked on as foremost among those deserving of alms; embracing and upholding the correct Dharma, he gave guidance to old and young. In a spirit of trust and harmony he conducted all kinds of business enterprises, but though he reaped worldly profits, he took no delight in these.

He frequented the busy crossroads in order to bring benefit to others, entered the government offices and courts of law so as to aid and rescue all those he could. He visited the places of debate in order to guide others to the Great Vehicle, visited the schools and study halls to further the instruction of the pupils. He entered houses of ill fame to teach the folly of fleshly desire, entered wine shops in order to encourage those with a will to quit them.

If he was among rich men, they honored him as foremost among them because he preached the superior Law for them. If

---

1. *This paragraph describes Vimalakirti's practice of the six paramitas, for which see glossary.*

he was among lay believers, they honored him as foremost because he freed them from greed and attachment. Among Kshatriyas he was most highly honored because he taught them forbearance. Among Brahmans he was most highly honored because he rid them of their self-conceit. The great ministers honored him as foremost because he taught the correct Law. The princes honored him as foremost because he showed them how to be loyal and filial. Within the women's quarters he was most honored because he converted and brought refinement to the women of the harem.

The common people honored him as first among them because he helped them to gain wealth and power. The Brahma deities honored him as first among them because he revealed the superiority of wisdom. The Indras honored him as first among them because he demonstrated the truth of impermanence. The Four Heavenly Kings, guardians of the world, honored him as foremost because he guarded all living beings.

In this way the rich man Vimalakirti employed immeasurable numbers of expedient means in order to bring benefit to others.

Using these expedient means, he made it appear that his body had fallen prey to illness. Because of his illness, the king of the country, the great ministers, rich men, lay believers, and Brahmans, as well as the princes and lesser officials, numbering countless thousands, all went to see him and inquire about his illness.

Vimalakirti then used this bodily illness to expound the Law to them in broad terms: "Good people, this body is impermanent, without durability, without strength, without firmness, a thing that decays in a moment, not to be relied on. It suffers, it is tormented, a meeting place of manifold ills.

"Good people, no person of enlightened wisdom could depend on a thing like this body. This body is like a cluster of foam, nothing you can grasp or handle. This body is like a bubble that cannot continue for long. This body is like a flame born of longing and desire. This body is like the plantain that has no firmness in its trunk. This body is like a phantom, the product of error and confusion. This body is like a dream, compounded of false and empty visions. This body is like a shadow, appearing through karma causes. This body is like an echo, tied to causes and conditions. This body is like a drifting cloud, changing and vanishing in an instant. This body is like lightning, barely lasting from moment to moment.

"This body is like earth that has no subjective being. This body is like fire, devoid of ego. This body is like wind that has no set life span. This body is like water, devoid of individuality.

"This body has no reality but makes these four elements its lodging. This body is void, removed from self and self's possessions. This body is without understanding, like plants or trees, tiles or pebbles. This body is without positive action, blown about by the wind. This body is impure, crammed with defilement and evil. This body is empty and unreal; though for a time you may bathe and cleanse, clothe and feed it, in the end it must crumble and fade. This body is plague-ridden, beset by a hundred and one ills and anxieties. This body is like the abandoned well on the hillside, old age pressing in on it. This body has no fixity, but is destined for certain death. This body is like poisonous snakes, vengeful bandits, or an empty village, a mere coming together of components, realms, and sense-fields.

"Good people, a thing like this is irksome and hateful, and therefore you should seek the Buddha body. Why? Because the Buddha body is the Dharma body. It is born from immeasurable merits and wisdom. It is born from precepts, meditation, wisdom, emancipation, and the insight of emancipation. It is born from pity, compassion, joy, and indifference. It is born of the various paramitas such as almsgiving, keeping of the precepts, forbearance and gentleness, assiduousness in religious practice, meditation, emancipation and samadhi, wide knowledge and wisdom. It is born of expedient means, born of the six transcen-

35

dental powers, born of the three understandings, born of the thirty-seven elements of the Way, born of concentration and insight, born of the ten powers, the four kinds of fearlessness, and the eighteen unshared properties. It is born of the cutting off of all things not good and the gathering in of all good things, born of the truth, born of the avoidance of indulgence and laxity. The body of the Thus Come One is born of immeasurable numbers of pure and spotless things such as these.

"Good people, if you wish to gain the Buddha body and do away with the ills that afflict all living beings, then you must set your minds on attaining anuttara-samyak-sambodhi."

In this manner the rich man Vimalakirti used the occasion to preach the Law to those who came to inquire about his illness. As a result, numberless thousands of persons were all moved to set their minds on the attainment of anuttara-samyak-sambodhi.

*Chapter 3*

At that time the rich man Vimalakirti thought to himself: "I am lying here sick in bed. Why does the World-Honored One in his great compassion fail to show some concern for me?"

The Buddha, aware of this thought, said to Shariputra, "You must go visit Vimalakirti and inquire about his illness."

But Shariputra replied to the Buddha in these words: "World-Honored One, I am not competent to visit him and inquire about his illness. Why? Because I recall one occasion in the past when I was sitting in quiet meditation under a tree in the forest.

"At that time Vimalakirti approached and said to me, 'Ah, Shariputra, you should not assume that this sort of sitting is true quiet sitting! Quiet sitting means that in this threefold world you manifest neither body nor will. This is quiet sitting. Not rising out of your samadhi of complete cessation and yet showing yourself in the ceremonies of daily life—this is quiet sitting. Not abandoning the principles of the Way and yet showing yourself in the activities of a common mortal—this is quiet sitting. Your mind not fixed on internal things and yet not engaged with externals either—this is quiet sitting. Unmoved by sundry theories, but practicing the thirty-seven elements of the Way—this is quiet sitting. Entering nirvana without having put an end to earthly desires—this is quiet sitting. If you can do this kind of sitting, you will merit the Buddha's seal of approval.'

"At that time, World-Honored One, when I heard him speak these words, I remained silent, for I had no way to reply to them. That is why I am not competent to visit him and inquire about his illness."

37

The Buddha then said to Maudgalyayana, "You must go visit Vimalakirti and inquire about his illness."

But Maudgalyayana replied to the Buddha: "World-Honored One, I am not competent to visit him and inquire about his illness. Why? Because I recall how in the past I entered the great city of Vaishali and in its streets and lanes expounded the Dharma for the lay believers.

"At that time Vimalakirti approached and said to me, 'Ah, Maudgalyayana, when you expound the Dharma for the white-robed lay believers, you should not expound it the way you are doing! Expounding the Dharma should be done in accordance with the Dharma [reality] itself.

" 'The Dharma knows nothing of living beings, because it is removed from the defilement of such concepts as "living beings." The Dharma knows nothing of "I," because it is removed from the defilement of such concepts as "I." It knows nothing of a life span, because it knows nothing of birth and death. It knows nothing of individuality, because it is cut off from considerations of past or future lives. The Dharma is forever still and serene, because it has wiped out all characteristics. The Dharma is without characteristics, because it is without anything that can be perceived. The Dharma is without names or appellations, because it is cut off from all language. The Dharma is without any expounding, because it is removed from broad or minute contemplation by the mind. The Dharma is without forms or characteristics, because it is as though vacant and empty. The Dharma is not the subject of frivolous theories, because in the end it is empty. The Dharma is without the concept of "mine," because it is removed from all such concepts of personal possession. The Dharma is without distinctions, because it is apart from all types of consciousness. The Dharma has nothing it can compare to, because there is no entity that can be set beside it.

" 'The Dharma is not affected by causes, because it does not exist in a conditioned realm. The Dharma is identical with the

Dharma-nature, because it enters into all phenomena [dharmas]. The Dharma conforms with what is truly so, because there is nothing else to conform to. The Dharma abides in the locus of reality, being unaffected by anything on the periphery. The Dharma is without motion or wavering, never depending on the six sense objects. The Dharma is without coming or going, since it never abides anywhere to begin with.

" 'The Dharma accords with emptiness, follows what is formless, responds to what is actionless. The Dharma is separate from beautiful or ugly. The Dharma knows no increase or diminution, the Dharma knows no birth or extinction, the Dharma knows no destination. The Dharma transcends eyes, ears, nose, tongue, body, and mind. The Dharma knows no high or low. The Dharma constantly abides without moving. The Dharma is separate from all meditational practices.

" 'Ah, Maudgalyayana, since the characteristics of the Dharma are such as these, how can one expound it? Expounding the Dharma means no expounding, no demonstrating, and listening to the Dharma means no listening, no grasping. It is like a conjurer of phantoms expounding the Dharma for phantom persons. It is with this understanding that you should expound the Dharma.

" 'You should take into account that some living beings are keen in capacity while others are dull, cultivate the kind of skilled insight that is free from all impediment, with a mind steeped in great compassion praise the Great Vehicle, and remember the debt of gratitude you owe the Buddha, never allowing the Three Treasures to come to an end. When you have done all this, then you may expound the Dharma.'

"When Vimalakirti expounded the Dharma in this way, eight hundred lay believers set their minds on the attainment of anuttara-samyak-sambodhi. I possess no such eloquence as this. Therefore I say that I am not competent to visit him and inquire about his illness."

The Buddha then said to Mahakashyapa, "You must go visit Vimalakirti and inquire about his illness."

But Mahakashyapa replied to the Buddha: "World-Honored One, I am not competent to visit him and inquire about his illness. Why? Because I recall how in the past I was begging for alms in a poor village.

"At that time Vimalakirti approached and said to me, 'Ah, Mahakashyapa, you have a mind marked by compassion and pity, but you do not know how to apply it to all alike. Instead you shun the rich and mighty and beg alms among the poor.

" 'Mahakashyapa, you must abide by the principle of equanimity and in that spirit go about begging for food. Because in the end there is no such thing as eating, in that spirit one goes about begging for food. Because one wishes to destroy dependence on things characterized by a mere combination of elements, in that spirit one accepts these balls of foodstuff. Because in the end there is no receiving, in that spirit one receives this food.

" 'When you enter a village, think of it as an empty village. The forms you see there should appear as they would to a blind man, the sounds you hear should be mere echoes. The aromas you inhale should be so much thin air, the flavors you taste should be undifferentiated.

" 'Accept all sensations in accordance with the enlightenment of wisdom, and understand that all phenomena are no more than phantom forms. They have no intrinsic nature, nor do they take on any other nature.[1]

" 'Mahakashyapa, if, without casting aside the eight errors, you can enter into the eight emancipations; if, while possessing the marks of error, you can enter the correct Law; if with one meal you can feed all beings, offering alms to the Buddhas

---

1. Or, according to another interpretation: "Intrinsically they have never been on fire, and hence will never burn out." The character jan can mean either "so," or "thus," or "to burn."

and the sages and worthy persons, then after that you may eat your food.

" 'One who eats in this manner neither possesses earthly desires nor is separated from earthly desires, neither enters into a meditative state of mind nor arises out of such a state, neither dwells in this world nor dwells in nirvana.

" 'One who gives alms in this manner derives neither great fortune nor little fortune, neither profit nor loss. This is the correct way to enter the Buddha way without relying on the path of the voice-hearer.

" 'Mahakashyapa, if you can eat your food in this manner, then you will not be eating in vain the food that others give you.'

"At that time, World-Honored One, when I heard him speak these words, I gained what I had never had before, and I was inspired with a profound respect for all the bodhisattvas. And I thought to myself, 'If this householder possesses such eloquence and wisdom that he can speak like this, then who could listen to him without being moved to set his mind on the attainment of anuttara-samyak-sambodhi?' From that time on I ceased to urge others to follow the path of the voice-hearer or the pratyekabuddha. That is why I say I am not competent to visit him and inquire about his illness."

The Buddha then said to Subhuti, "You must go visit Vimalakirti and inquire about his illness."

But Subhuti replied to the Buddha: "World-Honored One, I am not competent to visit him and ask about his illness. Why? Because I recall how in the past I went to his house to beg alms.

"At that time Vimalakirti took my begging bowl, filled it with things to eat, and said, 'Ah, Subhuti, if one can look on all foods as equal, that person can look on all things as equal, and if one looks on all things as equal, one will look on all foods as equal. If one begs alms in this manner, then one is worthy to receive food.

" 'Subhuti, if you can not cut yourself off from lewdness, anger, and stupidity and yet not be a part of these; if you can refrain from destroying the idea of a self and yet see all things as of a single nature; if without wiping out stupidity and attachment you can find your way to understanding and freedom from attachment; if you can seem to be a perpetrator of the five cardinal sins and yet gain emancipation; if you can be neither unbound nor bound, neither one who has perceived the four noble truths nor one who has not perceived them, neither one who obtains the fruits of religious practice nor one who does not obtain them, neither a common mortal nor one who has removed himself from the ways of the common mortal, neither a sage nor not a sage—if in this manner you can master all phenomenal things and yet remove yourself from the ways that mark them, then you will be worthy to receive food.

" 'Subhuti, if without seeing the Buddha or listening to his Law you are willing to take those six heretical teachers, Purana Kashyapa, Maskarin Goshaliputra, Samjayin Vairatiputra, Ajita Keshakambala, Kakuda Katyayana, and Nirgrantha Jnatiputra, as your teachers, leave the household life because of them, and follow them in falling into the same errors they fall into, then you will be worthy to receive food.

" 'Subhuti, if you can subscribe to erroneous views and thus never reach the "other shore" of enlightenment; if you can remain among the eight difficulties and never escape from difficulty, and can make common cause with earthly desires and remove yourself from a state of purity; if when you attain the samadhi of nondisputation you allow all living beings to attain the same degree of concentration; if those who give you alms are not destined to gain good fortune thereby, and those who make offerings to you fall into the three evil paths of existence; if you are willing to join hands with the host of devils and make the defilements your companion; if you can be no different from all these devils and these dusts and defilements; if you can bear hatred toward all living beings, slander the Buddhas, vilify the Law, not be counted among the assembly of monks, and in the end never attain nirvana—if you can do all this, then you will be worthy to receive food.'

"At that time, World-Honored One, when I heard these words, I was dumbfounded, not knowing what sort of words they were or how to answer them. I put down my alms bowl, intending to leave the house, but Vimalakirti said to me, 'Ah, Subhuti, pick up your alms bowl and do not be afraid. Why do I say this? If some phantom person conjured up by the Thus Come One were to reprimand you as I have just done, you would not be afraid, would you?'

" 'No,' I replied.

"Vimalakirti said, 'All things in the phenomenal world are just such phantoms and conjured beings. So you have no cause to feel afraid. Why? Because all words and pronouncements too are no different from these other phantom forms. When a person is wise, he does not cling to words and hence is not afraid of them. Why? Because words are something apart from self-nature—words do not really exist. And this is emancipation. All things of the phenomenal world bear this mark of emancipation.'

"When Vimalakirti expounded the Law in this manner, two hundred heavenly beings gained the purity of the Dharma eye. Therefore I say I am not competent to visit him and ask about his illness."

The Buddha then said to Purna Maitrayaniputra, "You must go visit Vimalakirti and ask about his illness."

43

But Purna said to the Buddha, "World-Honored One, I am not competent to visit him and ask about his illness. Why? Because I recall how once, under a tree in the great forest, I was expounding the Law to some monks who had just begun their study of the Way.

"At that time Vimalakirti approached and said to me, 'Ah, Purna, you should first enter into meditation and observe a person's mind before expounding the Law to that person. One does not put rotten food in a precious vessel. You must determine what thoughts are in the minds of these monks. Do not treat precious lapis lazuli as though it were mere glass!

" 'You seem unable to understand the basic capacities of living beings. You must not try to rouse their aspirations by preaching the doctrines of the Lesser Vehicle. Do not inflict injury on those who are without wounds! If you want them to travel the great highway, do not show them a little bypath. Do not try to fit the vast ocean into an ox's hoofprint, do not regard the light of the sun as if it were a firefly's glimmer!

" 'Purna, these monks long ago set their minds on the Great Vehicle, but later they forgot their original intentions. Why do you use the doctrines of the Lesser Vehicle to teach and guide them? As I see it, the wisdom of the Lesser Vehicle is trite and shallow, like the understanding of a blind person. It is incapable of discerning whether the capacities of living beings are keen or dull.'

"At that time Vimalakirti entered into samadhi, making it possible for these monks to become aware of their former existences. In the past, under five hundred Buddhas, they had planted the roots of virtue and set their minds on the attainment of anuttara-samyak-sambodhi. And at that moment they were suddenly able to regain their original spirit of resolve. With that, the monks bowed their heads at Vimalakirti's feet. Then he preached the Law for them, insuring that they would never again regress in their striving for anuttara-samyak-sambodhi. And I thought to myself that a voice-hearer should never preach the Law when he cannot discern people's inner capacities. Therefore I say I am not competent to visit Vimalakirti and inquire about his illness."

The Buddha then said to Mahakatyayana, "You must go visit Vimalakirti and ask about his illness."

But Mahakatyayana said to the Buddha, "World-Honored One, I am not competent to visit him and ask about his illness. Why? Because I recall how in the past the Buddha was once summing up for the monks the essential points in his preaching of the Law. Later, I expounded and elaborated on what he had said, discussing the meaning of the terms impermanence, suffering, emptiness, non-ego, and tranquil extinction or nirvana.

"At that time Vimalakirti approached and said to me, 'Ah, Mahakatyayana, you must not try to expound on the true nature of phenomena when your mind is concerned with distinctions such as birth or extinction. For in the end all phenomena know neither birth nor extinction—this is the meaning of impermanence. The five components are wide open, empty, nothing arising in them—this is the meaning of suffering. The various phenomena ultimately have no existence—this is the meaning of emptiness. Ego and non-ego are not two different things—this is the meaning of non-ego. Phenomena have never been "so" to begin with, and hence will never cease to be "so"[2]— this is the meaning of tranquil extinction.'

"When he expounded the Law in this way, the minds of the monks were able to gain emancipation. That is why I say I am not competent to visit Vimalakirti and ask about his illness."

The Buddha then said to Aniruddha, "You must go visit Vimalakirti and ask about his illness."

But Aniruddha said to the Buddha, "World-Honored One, I am not competent to visit him and ask about his illness. Why? Because I recall how once I was walking around to stretch my legs when a Brahma king named Austere Purity, accompanied by ten thousand Brahmas, all emitting beams of pure light, came to the place where I was. Bowing his head in obeisance, he questioned me, saying, 'Aniruddha, how far can this divine eye of yours see?'[3]

45

2. *Or, according to another interpretation: "Things have never been on fire to begin with, so they cannot go out now." See note 1 in this chapter.*
3. *Aniruddha was known among the ten major disciples as foremost in divine sight.*

"I replied, 'Sir, I can see this whole thousand-millionfold world, the Buddha land of Shakyamuni, as though I were peering down at a myrobalan fruit in the palm of my hand.'

"At that time Vimalakirti approached and said to me, 'Ah, Aniruddha, this sight possessed by the divine eye—is it conditioned in nature, or is it unconditioned? If it is conditioned in nature, then it is the same as the five transcendental powers of the non-Buddhist teachers. And if it is unconditioned, then it is uncreated, and hence is incapable of seeing anything.'

"At that time I remained silent. But the Brahmas, hearing his words, gained what they had never had before. At once they made obeisance to him and said, 'In this world, who possesses the true divine eye?'

"Vimalakirti replied, 'Only the Buddha, the World-Honored One, is able to acquire the true divine eye. He is constantly in a state of samadhi and can see all the Buddha lands, because he does not see in terms of duality.'

"Thereupon the Brahma king Austere Purity and his retinue of five hundred Brahma deities all set their minds on the attainment of anuttara-samyak-sambodhi. They bowed at Vimalakirti's feet and then suddenly were seen no more. Therefore I say I am not competent to visit Vimalakirti and ask about his illness.'

The Buddha then said to Upali, "You must go visit Vimalakirti and ask about his illness."

But Upali replied to the Buddha, "World-Honored One, I am not competent to visit him and ask about his illness. Why? Because I recall once in the past when two monks had violated the rules of conduct and were feeling ashamed of themselves but did not dare ask the Buddha what to do. So they came to me and said, 'Ah, Upali, we have violated the precepts and are truly ashamed, but we do not dare ask the Buddha what to do. Please free us from our doubts and remorse and tell us how we can be excused from blame.'[4]

4. *Upali was known as foremost in observing the precepts.*

"I explained to them how one goes about gaining pardon according to the Law. But at that time Vimalakirti approached and said to me, 'Ah, Upali, do not make the offense these monks have committed even worse than it is! You should go about wiping out their doubts and remorse at once and not trouble their minds further!

" 'Why do I say this? Because their offense by its nature does not exist either inside them, or outside, or in between. As the Buddha has taught us, when the mind is defiled, the living being will be defiled. When the mind is pure, the living being will be pure. As the mind is, so will be the offense or defilement. The same is true of all things, for none escape the realm of Suchness.

" 'Now, Upali, if one gains emancipation from delusion through an understanding of the nature of the mind, does any defilement remain?'

" 'No,' I replied.

"Vimalakirti said, 'In the same way, when all living beings gain an understanding of the nature of the mind, then no defilement exists. Ah, Upali, deluded thoughts are defilement. Where there are no deluded thoughts, that is purity. Topsy-turvy thinking is defilement. Where there is no topsy-turvy thinking, that is purity. Belief in the self is defilement. Where there is no such belief, that is purity.

" 'Upali, all phenomena are born and pass into extinction, never enduring, like phantoms, like lightning. They do not wait for one another or linger for an instant. All phenomena are the product of deluded vision, like dreams, like flames, like the moon in the water or an image in a mirror, born of deluded thoughts. One who understands this is called a keeper of the precepts, one who understands this is called well liberated.'

"At this, the two monks exclaimed, 'Superlative wisdom! Upali could never match this; he who is "foremost in observing the precepts" could never speak like this!' And I added, 'Leaving the Thus Come One aside, no voice-hearer or bodhisattva has

47

ever commanded such eloquence in apt exposition. See how clear and penetrating his wisdom is!'

"At that time the doubts and remorse of the two monks were wiped away and they set their minds on the attainment of anuttara-samyak-sambodhi, vowing that 'We will enable all living beings to gain eloquence such as this!' Therefore I say I am not competent to visit Vimalakirti and ask about his illness."

The Buddha then said to Rahula, "You must go visit Vimalakirti and ask about his illness."

But Rahula said to the Buddha, "World-Honored One, I am not competent to visit him and ask about his illness. Why? Because I recall how once in the past the sons of the wealthy men of Vaishali came to the place where I was, bowed their heads in obeisance, and questioned me. 'Ah, Rahula,' they said, 'you are the Buddha's son, but you cast aside your claim to the rank of a wheel-turning king and left the household life to become a monk. What benefits does one acquire by leaving the household life?'

"I explained to them the benefits and blessings one gains by leaving the household life as the Law describes them. But at that time Vimalakirti approached and said to me, 'Ah, Rahula, you should not speak of the benefits and blessings gained by leaving the household life. Why? Because to be without benefits and without blessings is to leave household life.

" 'In the case of things that are conditioned in nature one may speak of them as having benefits and blessings. But one who leaves household life enters the realm of the unconditioned, and in the realm of the unconditioned there are no benefits, no blessings.

" 'Rahula, leaving the household life is not that, not this, and not in between. It means abandoning the sixty-two erroneous views to reside in nirvana; it is accepted by the wise and carried out by the sages. It means conquering and subduing the host of devils, moving beyond the five realms of existence, purifying the five eyes, acquiring the five powers, and cultivating the five roots of goodness. It means not troubling others but removing oneself from sundry evils, refuting the non-Buddhist doctrines, transcending the realm of makeshift names, shaking off mud and defilement. It is without ties or attachments, without personal possessions, without thought of possessions, without fluster or confusion. It means harboring joy within, guarding the minds of others, pursuing the practice of meditation, and freeing oneself from all fault. If one can do all this, then one has truly left the household.'

"Then Vimalakirti addressed the rich men's sons, saying, 'Now that you are in the midst of the correct Law, you should all join in leaving the household life. Why? Because it is rare to happen on a time when the Buddha is in the world!'

"But the rich men's sons said, 'Layman, we have heard the Buddha say that one must not leave the household life without the permission of one's parents.'

" 'In that case, you should set your minds on attaining anuttara-samyak-sambodhi,' said Vimalakirti. 'That is the same as leaving the household, the same as taking monastic vows.'

"At that time thirty-two rich men's sons all set their minds on attaining anuttara-samyak-sambodhi. Therefore I say I am not competent to visit Vimalakirti and ask about his illness."

The Buddha then said to Ananda, "You must go visit Vimalakirti and ask about his illness."

But Ananda said to the Buddha, "World-Honored One, I am not competent to visit him and ask about his illness. Why? Because I recall once in the past when the World-Honored One was feeling somewhat ill and needed some cow's milk. I at once took my begging bowl, went to the home of one of the great Brahmans, and stood by the gate. At that time Vimalakirti approached and said to me, 'Ah, Ananda, what are you doing standing here early in the morning with your begging bowl?'

"I replied, 'Layman, the World-Honored One is suffering from a slight bodily illness and needs some cow's milk. That's why I've come here.'

"But Vimalakirti said, 'Hush, hush, Ananda! Never speak such words! The body of the Thus Come One is diamond-hard in substance. All evils have been cut away, manifold good things gather there. How could it know illness, how could it know distress? Go your way in silence, Ananda, and do not defame the Thus Come One. Don't let others hear you speaking such coarse words! Don't let these heavenly beings of great majesty and virtue and these bodhisattvas who have come from the pure lands of other regions hear such utterances!

" 'Ananda, even a wheel-turning sage king with his few blessings is still able to exempt himself from illness. How much more so, then, the Thus Come One, in whom immeasurable blessings meet, the surpasser of all! Be on your way, Ananda, and do not inflict this shame on us.

" 'If the non-Buddhists and Brahmans should hear such talk, they would think to themselves: "Why call this man Teacher? He cannot save himself from illness, so how could he save others from their illnesses?" Slip away quickly now so no one will hear what you have said!

" 'Ananda, you should know that the body of the Thus Come One is the Dharma body, not the body of the world of thought and desires. The Buddha is the World-Honored One who transcends the threefold world. The Buddha body is free of outflows, for all its outflows have been cut off. The Buddha body is unconditioned and does not fall within the realm of destinies. A body such as this—how could it know illness, how could it know distress?'

"At that time, World-Honored One, I felt truly ashamed and thought, I must go to the Buddha and ask if I heard him incorrectly. But at that moment I heard a voice in the sky saying, 'Ananda, it is as the layman has said. But the Buddha has appeared in this evil world of five impurities and at present is practicing the Law so as to save and liberate living beings. Go, Ananda, get the milk and do not feel ashamed!'

"But, World-Honored One, Vimalakirti commands such wisdom and eloquence as this! That is why I say I am not competent to visit him and ask about his illness."

Thus all five hundred of the major disciples one by one described to the Buddha some earlier experience and the words that Vimalakirti had spoken on that occasion, each declaring, "I am not competent to visit him and ask about his illness."

## Chapter 4

## THE BODHISATTVAS

The Buddha then said to the bodhisattva Maitreya, "You must go visit Vimalakirti and inquire about his illness."

But Maitreya replied to the Buddha: "World-Honored One, I am not competent to visit him and inquire about his illness. Why? Because I recall how once in the past I was preaching to the king of the Tushita heaven and his followers on the practices required to attain the state of nonregression.

"At that time Vimalakirti approached and said to me, 'Maitreya, the World-Honored One prophesied that with one more birth you will be able to attain anuttara-samyak-sambodhi. Now just what birth does this prophecy apply to? Does it apply to your past birth, your future birth, or your present birth?

" 'If it applies to a past birth, that past birth has already passed into extinction. If it applies to a future birth, that future birth has yet to arrive. And if it applies to a present birth, this present birth lacks permanence. For, as the Buddha has said, "Monks, one moment you are born, the next you grow old, the next you pass into extinction.'

" 'Or does the prophecy apply to the state of birthlessness? But birthlessness is none other than the state of Correct Realization, and the stage of Correct Realization can have nothing to do with prophecies of enlightenment or with the attainment of anuttara-samyak-sambodhi. So how, Maitreya, can you be given this prophecy about "one birth"?

" 'Were you given this prophecy because of some birth that pertains to Suchness? Or were you given this prophecy because of some extinction that pertains to Suchness? If you were given this prophecy because of some birth that pertains to Suchness, you should know that in Suchness there is no birth. And if you were given this prophecy because of some extinction that pertains to Suchness, you should know that in Suchness there is no extinction.

" 'All living beings are a part of Suchness, and all other things as well are a part of Suchness. The sages and worthy ones too are a part of Suchness; even you, Maitreya, are a part of Suchness. So if you have been given a prophecy of enlightenment, then all living beings should likewise be given such a prophecy. Why? Because Suchness knows no dualism or differentiation. If you, Maitreya, are able to attain anuttara-samyak-sambodhi, then all living beings should likewise be able to attain it. Why? Because all living beings in truth bear the marks of bodhi. If you, Maitreya, are able to gain nirvana, then all living beings should likewise be able to gain it. Why? Because the Buddhas know that all living beings bear the marks of tranquil extinction, which is nirvana, and that there is no further extinction. Therefore, Maitreya, you must not use doctrines such as this to mislead these offspring of the gods. For in truth there is no such thing as setting one's mind on the attainment of anuttara-samyak-sambodhi or of attaining the state of nonregression.

" 'Maitreya, you should persuade these offspring of the gods to abandon any view that makes distinctions concerning bodhi. Why? Because bodhi is not something that can be acquired by the body, or acquired by the mind.

" 'Tranquil extinction is bodhi, for in it all marks become extinct. Noncontemplation is bodhi, for it is divorced from all causes. Nonaction is bodhi, for it is devoid of thought and mental activity. Cutting off is bodhi, for it abandons all views. Removal is bodhi, for it means the removal of all deluded thoughts.

" 'Blocking is bodhi, because it blocks out all aspiration. Noninvolvement is bodhi, because it is without greed or attachment. Compliance is bodhi, because it complies with Suchness. Abiding is bodhi, because it abides in the Dharma-nature.

" 'Extending is bodhi, for it extends to the limit of reality. Nonduality is bodhi, for it is removed from thoughts and thought objects. Equality is bodhi, for in it all is equally empty and void. The unconditioned is bodhi, for it knows no birth, abiding, or extinction. Understanding is bodhi, for it fully comprehends the mental activities of living beings.

"Nonengagement is bodhi, because it enters into no kind of engagement with objects. Nonparticipation is bodhi, because it has freed itself from the habits of earthly desire. The dwellingless is bodhi, because it lacks shape or form. The provisionally named is bodhi, because names and words are void.

" 'Phantomlike is bodhi, for it neither grasps nor lets go. Untroubled is bodhi, for it is forever still of itself. Good tranquillity[1] is bodhi, for it is pure in nature. Ungrasping is bodhi, for it is removed from distracting causes. Nondifferentiation is bodhi, for in it all phenomena are equal. Incomparable is bodhi, for no simile can convey it. Subtle and wonderful is bodhi, for phenomena are hard to understand.'

"World-Honored One, when Vimalakirti expounded the Law in this fashion, two hundred offspring of the gods were able to grasp the truth of birthlessness. Therefore I say I am not competent to visit him and ask about his illness."

The Buddha then said to the bodhisattva Shining Adornment, a young boy, "You must go visit Vimalakirti and ask about his illness."

But Shining Adornment replied to the Buddha: "World-Honored One, I am not competent to visit him and inquire about his illness. Why? Because I remember once in the past when I was leaving the great city of Vaishali. Vimalakirti was just then entering the city, and I accordingly bowed to him and said, 'Layman, where are you coming from?'

"He replied, 'I am coming from the place of practice.'

---

1. *Some texts read "The tranquillity of meditation."*

" 'The place of practice—where is that?' I asked.

"He replied, 'An upright mind is the place of practice, for it is without sham or falsehood. The resolve to act is the place of practice, for it can judge matters properly. A deeply searching mind is the place of practice, for it multiplies benefits. The mind that aspires to bodhi is the place of practice, for it is without error or misconception.

" 'Almsgiving is the place of practice, because it hopes for no reward. Observance of the precepts is the place of practice, because it brings fulfillment of vows. Forbearance is the place of practice, because it enables one to view all living beings with a mind free of obstruction. Assiduousness is the place of practice, because it forestalls laziness and regression. Meditation is the place of practice, because it makes the mind tame and gentle. Wisdom is the place of practice, because it sees all things as they are.

" 'Pity is the place of practice, for it views all living beings equally. Compassion is the place of practice, for it bears up under weariness and pain. Joy is the place of practice, for it revels in Dharma delight. Indifference is the place of practice, for it rejects both hatred and love.

" 'Transcendental powers are the place of practice, because thereby one masters the six powers. Emancipation is the place of practice, because it knows how to renounce and set aside. Expedient means are the place of practice, because they can teach and convert living beings. The four methods of winning people are the place of practice, because they can win living beings over. Much learning is the place of practice, because one carries out what one has learned. A disciplined mind is the place of practice, because one can thereby contemplate all phenomena correctly. The thirty-seven elements of the Way are the place of practice, because through them one rejects what is conditioned. Truth[2] is the place of practice, because it does not deceive the world.

2. *Some texts read "The four noble truths."*

" 'Causes and conditions are the place of practice, for none of the links in the chain of causation, from ignorance to old age and death, ever come to an end. Earthly desires are the place of practice, for through them we know the nature of Suchness. Living beings are the place of practice, for through them we know that there is no ego. All phenomena are the place of practice, for through them we know the emptiness of all phenomena.

" 'Conquering devils is the place of practice, because one is unswayed, unflinching. The threefold world is the place of practice, because there is no path for one there. The lion's roar is the place of practice, because it has nothing it fears. The ten powers, the four kinds of fearlessness, the eighteen unshared properties are the place of practice, because they are free of all fault. The three understandings are the place of practice, because they are without the least obstruction. Understanding all phenomena in one instant of thought is the place of practice, because one thereby becomes master of all wisdom.

" 'My good fellow, if bodhisattvas apply themselves to the paramitas and teach and convert living beings, then you should understand that everything they do, every lifting of a foot, every placing of a foot, will in effect be a "coming from the place of practice," an abiding in the Buddha's Law.'

"When Vimalakirti preached the Law in this manner, five hundred heavenly and human beings all set their minds on attaining anuttara-samyak-sambodhi. Therefore I say I am not competent to visit him and ask about his illness."

The Buddha then said to the bodhisattva Upholder of the Age, "You must go visit Vimalakirti and ask about his illness."

But Upholder of the Age said to the Buddha: "World-Honored One, I am not competent to visit him and inquire about his illness. Why? Because I recall once when I was staying in my quiet room. At that time the devil king Papiyas, accompanied by twelve thousand heavenly maidens, appeared in the guise of the god Indra. Playing on musical instruments and singing, they came to where I was, and then the devil and his retinue bowed their heads at my feet, pressed their palms together, and stood to one side.

"I thought it was Indra, and I said to him, 'Welcome, Kaushi-ka.[3] Though you enjoy good fortune, you should never behave willfully. You should contemplate the impermanence of the five desires and strive thereby to plant good roots. With body, life, and resources you should cultivate the steadfast Law.'

"But Indra said to me, 'Upright one, please accept these twelve thousand heavenly maidens. They can serve and wait on you.'

"I replied, 'Kaushika, a monk, a son of Shakyamuni, has no use for unlawful things such as these. It would not be right for me to accept them.'

"Before I had finished speaking, Vimalakirti approached and said to me, 'This is not Indra. This is only a devil who has come to trouble and vex you.' Then he said to the devil, 'You may give these women to me. It is quite all right for me to accept them.'

"The devil was alarmed and fearful, thinking that Vimalakirti was perhaps going to make trouble for him. He tried to hide himself and escape, but he could not make himself invisible. Though he exhausted all his supernatural powers, he could not get away.

"Just then a voice was heard in the sky saying, 'Papiyas, give him the women. Then you can escape.'

"The devil, terrified, looked this way and that and then handed over the women. Vimalakirti then addressed the women, saying, 'The devil has given you to me. Now it is proper that you should all set your minds on attaining anuttara-samyak-sambodhi.'

"Then, adopting whatever approach was appropriate, he expounded the Law to them, awakening in them a desire for the Way. Then he said, 'Now that you have conceived a desire for the Way, you may regale yourselves with Dharma delight and need no longer delight in the pleasures of the five desires.'

3. *Kaushika is another name for Indra.*

"The heavenly maidens asked, 'What is this you call Dharma delight?'

"Vimalakirti replied, 'To delight in constant faith in the Buddha, to delight in the desire to hear the Law, to delight in giving alms to the assembly, to delight in casting off the five desires, to delight in viewing the five components as vengeful bandits, to delight in viewing the four great elements as poisonous snakes, to delight in viewing the mind and the senses as an empty village, to delight in pursuing and guarding a desire for the Way, to delight in benefiting living beings, to delight in honoring and supporting teachers, to delight in practicing widespread generosity, to delight in strict observance of the precepts, to delight in patience, humility, gentleness, and harmony, to delight in diligently amassing good roots, to delight in meditation that is never disordered, to delight in bright, undefiled wisdom, to delight in broadening the mind that aspires to bodhi, to delight in conquering and subduing devils, to delight in cutting off all earthly desires, to delight in purifying the Buddha lands, to delight in gaining merits so that one may in time succeed in acquiring auspicious marks and characteristics, to delight in adorning the place of practice, to delight in listening fearlessly to profound teachings, to delight in the three gates to emancipation and not to delight in untimely teachings, to delight in being friendly with those of like learning, to delight in a mind free of anger and hostility when among those of unlike learning, to delight in guiding and protecting evil friends, to delight in being friendly with good friends, to delight in a mind that finds joy in purity, to delight in practicing the teachings regarding the immeasurable elements of the Way—these make up the Dharma delight of the bodhisattva.'

"Papiyas then addressed the women, saying, 'I want now to return with you to my heavenly palace.' But the women said, 'You gave us to this layman. Possessing this Dharma delight that affords us such pleasure, we no longer delight in the pleasures of the five desires.'

"The devil said, 'Layman, you should give up these women. He who gives all he possesses as a gift to others is a bodhisattva.'

"Vimalakirti replied, 'I have already given them up. You may take them away, and may you enable all living beings to fulfill their desire for the Dharma!'

"But the women said to Vimalakirti, 'How can we remain in the palace of the devil?'

"Vimalakirti replied, 'Sisters, there is a teaching called the Inexhaustible Lamp. You must study it. This Inexhaustible Lamp is like a single lamp that lights a hundred or a thousand other lamps, till the darkness is all made bright with a brightness that never ends. In this same way, sisters, one bodhisattva guides and opens a path for a hundred or a thousand living beings, causing them to set their minds on attaining anuttara-samyak-sambodhi. And this desire for the Way will never be extinguished or go out. By following the teaching as it has been preached, one keeps adding until one has acquired all good teachings. This is what is called the Inexhaustible Lamp.

" 'Although you live in the palace of the devil, with this Inexhaustible Lamp you can enable countless heavenly sons and heavenly daughters to set their minds on attaining anuttara-samyak-sambodhi. Thus you will repay the debt of gratitude you owe the Buddha and at the same time bring great benefit to all living beings.'

"At that time the heavenly maidens bowed their heads at Vimalakirti's feet and then accompanied the devil back to his palace, suddenly disappearing from sight. World-Honored One, such are the freely commanded supernatural powers, wisdom, and eloquence that Vimalakirti possesses! Therefore I say I am not competent to visit him."

The Buddha then said to Good Virtue, one of the wealthy men's sons, "You must go visit Vimalakirti and ask about his illness."

But Good Virtue said to the Buddha, "World-Honored One, I am not competent to visit him and inquire about his illness.

Why? Because I recall once when a great bestowal gathering[4] was held at my father's house, where for a period of seven days alms were given out to all the monks, Brahmans and non-Buddhist believers, and to poor and humble folk, orphans, friendless persons and beggars.

"At that time Vimalakirti, who had joined the gathering, said to me, 'You are a wealthy man's son—you should not be holding a great bestowal gathering such as this. You should hold a gathering for Dharma bestowal. Why hold a gathering for the bestowal of mere material goods?'

" 'Layman,' I said, 'what do you mean by a gathering for Dharma bestowal?'

"He replied, 'A gathering for Dharma bestowal is one which has no beginning and no end, in which alms are given out simultaneously to all living beings. What does this mean? It means that through bodhi one cultivates a loving mind, through saving living beings one cultivates a mind of great compassion, through adherence to the correct Law one cultivates a joyful mind, and through one's grasp of wisdom one exercises an indifferent mind.

" 'By controlling stinginess and greed one carries out the paramita of *dana* or almsgiving, by converting those who violate the precepts one carries out the paramita of *shila* or keeping of the precepts, through the doctrine of no ego one carries out the paramita of *kshanti* or forbearance, by dispelling attachment to the characteristics of body and mind one carries out the paramita of *virya* or assiduousness, through an understanding of the nature of bodhi one carries out the paramita of *dhyana* or meditation, and through comprehensive wisdom one carries out the paramita of *prajna* or wisdom.

" 'By teaching and converting living beings one comes to understand emptiness, by not casting aside conditioned phe-

4. *A Brahmanical ceremony marked by sacrifices to the gods and the dispensing of charity to those pursuing the religious life and to needy persons.*

nomena one comes to understand formlessness, by recognizing that living beings take on visible form one comes to understand nonaction.

" 'By guarding and upholding the correct Law one acquires the power of expedient means, by rescuing living beings one acquires the four methods of winning people, by respecting and serving others one learns how to banish pride.

" 'With regard to body, life, and wealth, one follows the doctrine that these three are indestructible;[5] with regard to the six objects of reverence, one follows the method of thoughtful meditation; with regard to the six types of harmonious respect one cultivates a straightforward mind. By correctly practicing the good Law one achieves a pure way of life; through purity of mind, joy and delight one draws near to the worthy ones and sages; by not hating evil persons one learns to temper and discipline one's mind.

" 'By following the rules for those who have left the household life one cultivates a deeply searching mind; by carrying out religious practices in the prescribed way one acquires much learning; by observing ways that are free from contention one creates peaceful and uncrowded surroundings; by directing one's efforts toward Buddha wisdom one learns quiet meditation; by freeing living beings from their bonds one creates a setting for religious practice.

" 'Acquiring auspicious marks and purifying the Buddha lands, one pursues actions that bring blessing and good fortune; understanding the minds and thoughts of all living beings and preaching the Law to them in an appropriate manner, one pursues actions that bring wisdom; understanding that all phenomena are neither to be seized nor rejected, one enters the doctrinal gate of the single nature of all phenomena and pursues wise actions; cutting off all earthly desires, all blocks and hindrances,

5. *Not the ordinary body but the true or eternal body, etc.*

all doctrines that are not good, one pursues all manner of good works; acquiring all types of wisdom, all good doctrines, one cultivates all the methods that aid one to the Buddha way.[6]

" 'This, my good man, is what I mean by a gathering for Dharma bestowal. If one is a bodhisattva and abides in such a gathering for Dharma bestowal, he may be deemed a great donor of alms, and he will also be creating a field of blessings for all the world.'

"World-Honored One, when Vimalakirti expounded the Law in this fashion, two hundred of the Brahmans gathered there all set their minds on attaining anuttara-samyak-sambodhi. At that time my mind gained a purity I had never known before and I sighed with delight. Bowing my head in obeisance at the feet of Vimalakirti, I took off my jeweled necklace worth hundreds and thousands in gold and presented it to him, but he was unwilling to accept it.

" 'Layman,' I said, "I beg you by all means to accept this and to dispose of it as you wish.'

"Vimalakirti then accepted the necklace and divided it into two parts. One part he gave to the lowliest beggars in the assembly, and one part he presented to the Thus Come One Rarely Surpassed. At that time all the members of the gathering were able to see Thus Come One Rarely Surpassed in his land called Light Bright, and they could also see the necklace placed on his

---

6. *There are places in this troublesome passage where cause and effect seem to be in the reverse of their logical order; for example, one would expect the text to say that because one possesses a mind of great compassion, one seeks to save living beings, not that through saving living beings one acquires a mind of great compassion. But the Chinese seems to be saying the latter, and translations of the Tibetan version bear out this interpretation of the syntax throughout the passage. Note that Charles Luk, apparently in an effort to avoid such difficulties, in his translation of the Chinese (p. 46) arbitrarily reverses the order of cause and effect in the latter part of the passage.*

person. Then the necklace changed into a jeweled dias fitted with four pillars, richly adorned on four sides but without screens or obstructions enclosing it.

"Vimalakirti, having worked these supernatural wonders, then spoke these words: 'If a donor of alms bestows gifts on the lowliest beggars with equality of mind, dispensing them with impartiality as the Thus Come One does in his field of blessings; if one exercises great compassion in equal measure without seeking reward or recompense, this may be called a perfectly performed Dharma bestowal.'

"Then the lowliest beggars in the city, seeing these displays of supernatural power and hearing the words of doctrine that Vimalakirti had spoken, all set their minds on the attainment of anuttara-samyak-sambodhi. Therefore I say I am not competent to visit him and ask about his illness."

In this manner the various bodhisattvas one by one described to the Buddha some past encounter with Vimalakirti and praised the words he had spoken on that occasion, and all declared that they were not competent to visit him and ask about his illness.

## Chapter 5

INQUIRING ABOUT THE ILLNESS

At that time the Buddha said to Manjushri, "You must go visit Vimalakirti and inquire about his illness."

Manjushri replied to the Buddha, "World-Honored One, that eminent man is very difficult to confront. He is profoundly enlightened in the true nature of reality and skilled at preaching the essentials of the Law. His eloquence never falters, his wisdom is free of impediments. He understands all the rules of bodhisattva conduct, and nothing in the secret storehouse of the Buddhas is beyond his grasp. He has overcome the host of devils and disports himself with transcendental powers. In wisdom and expedient means he has mastered all there is to know. Nevertheless, in obedience to the Buddha's august command, I will go visit him and inquire about his illness."

Then the bodhisattvas and major disciples in the assembly, the Brahmas, Indras, and Four Heavenly Kings, all thought to themselves: "Now these two great men, Manjushri and Vimalakirti, will be talking together, and they will surely expound the wonderful Law!" At that time eight thousand bodhisattvas, five hundred voice-hearers, and hundreds and thousands of heavenly beings all decided at once that they would like to accompany Manjushri on his visit.

Manjushri, with this throng of bodhisattvas, major disciples, and heavenly beings reverently surrounding and accompanying him, proceeded to enter the city of Vaishali.

At that time the rich man Vimalakirti thought to himself, "Now Manjushri is coming with that great assembly!" At once he employed his supernatural powers to empty the room, clearing it of all its contents and his attendants, leaving only a single bed on which he lay in sickness.

When Manjushri entered the house, he saw that the room was bare of contents, with just one bed, Vimalakirti lying alone on it. Vimalakirti said, "Welcome, Manjushri! You come without the marks of coming, you see me without the marks of seeing me."

Manjushri said, "Just so, layman. What has already come can hardly be coming. And what has already departed can hardly be departing. What do I mean? What comes has nowhere it comes from, what departs has nowhere it goes, and what is seen cannot be further seen.[1] But let us put that aside for the moment.

"Layman, this illness of yours—can you endure it? Is the treatment perhaps not making it worse rather than better? The World-Honored One countless times has made solicitous inquiries concerning you. Layman, what is the cause of this illness? Has it been with you long? And how can it be cured?"

Vimalakirti replied, "This illness of mine is born of ignorance and feelings of attachment. Because all living beings are sick, therefore I am sick. If all living beings are relieved of sickness, then my sickness will be mended. Why? Because the bodhisattva for the sake of living beings enters the realm of birth and death, and because he is in the realm of birth and death he suffers illness. If living beings can gain release from illness, then the bodhisattva will no longer be ill.

"It is like the case of a rich man who has only one child. If the child falls ill, then the father and mother too will be ill, but if the child's illness is cured, the father and mother too will be cured. The bodhisattva is like this, for he loves living beings as though they were his children. If living beings are sick, the bodhisattva will be sick, but if living beings are cured, the bodhisattva too

65

---

1. *Vimalakirti and Manjushri do a brief pas de deux on the theme of nondualism before entering on their main dialogue.*

will be cured. You ask what cause this illness arises from—the illness of the bodhisattva arises from his great compassion."

Manjushri said, "Layman, why is this room empty and without attendants?"

Vimalakirti replied, "The lands of the Buddhas too are all empty."

"Why are they empty?"

"They are empty because of emptiness," Vimalakirti replied.

"And why is emptiness empty?" asked Manjushri.

"It is empty of distinctions, therefore it is empty," was the reply.

"Can emptiness itself be the subject of distinctions?" asked Manjushri.

"Distinctions too are empty," was the reply.

"How then is emptiness to be sought?" asked Manjushri.

"It may be sought in the sixty-two erroneous views of the non-Buddhists," was the reply.

"How are the sixty-two views to be sought?" asked Manjushri.

"They may be sought in the emancipation of the Buddhas," was the reply.

"And how is the emancipation of the Buddhas to be sought?" asked Manjushri.

66

"It may be sought in the minds and actions of all living beings," replied Vimalakirti. "And you asked why I am without attendants. But in fact the whole host of devils and the non-Buddhist believers are all my attendants. Why? Because the host of devils delight in the realm of birth and death, and while the bodhisattva is in the realm of birth and death he does not scorn their company. The non-Buddhist believers delight in various views of reality, and the bodhisattva knows how to remain unmoved by such views."

Manjushri said, "This illness of yours, layman—what form does it take?"

"My illness has no form," replied Vimalakirti. "It cannot be seen."

Manjushri said, "Is this illness seated in the body or in the mind?"

"It is not seated in the body, for it is apart from bodily form," replied Vimalakirti. "And it is not seated in the mind, for the mind is a phantomlike thing."

"Of the four major elements, earth, water, fire, and wind, to which of these elements does this illness pertain?" asked Manjushri.

Vimalakirti replied, "This illness does not pertain to the element earth, but neither is it separated from the element earth. And the same may be said of the elements water, fire, and wind. Yet the illnesses of living beings arise from the four elements. And because living beings have these illnesses, therefore I too am ill."

Then Manjushri asked Vimalakirti, "How should a bodhisattva go about comforting and instructing another bodhisattva who is ill?"

Vimalakirti replied, "Tell him about the impermanence of the body, but do not tell him to despise or turn away from the body. Tell him about the sufferings of the body, but do not tell him to strive for nirvana. Tell him that the body is without ego, but urge him to teach and guide living beings. Tell him of the emptiness of the body, but do not tell him of its final extinction. Tell him to repent of former offenses, but do not tell him to consign them to the past. Tell him to use his own illness as a means of sympathizing with the illness of others, for he should understand their sufferings throughout the countless kalpas of their past existence, and should think how he can bring benefit to all living beings. Tell him to recall the good fortune he has won through religious practice, to concentrate on a life of purity, and not to give way to gloom or worry. He should cultivate constant diligence, striving to become a king of physicians who can heal the ailments of the assembly. This is how a bodhisattva should comfort and instruct a bodhisattva who is ill so as to make him feel happy."

Manjushri said, "Layman, how should a bodhisattva who is ill go about tempering and controlling his mind?"

Vimalakirti replied, "A bodhisattva who is ill should think to himself: 'Now these illnesses of mine all spring from the deluded thoughts, the upside-down thinking and various earthly desires of my past existence. They have no real existence, so who is it who suffers illness? Why? The four major elements come together, and therefore we apply a makeshift name, calling the thing a body. But the four major elements have no master, and the body has no "I" or ego. And these illnesses too all arise from attachment to ego. Therefore I should harbor no such attachment to ego.'

"Once one has understood the origin of illness, one may do away with the thought of an I or ego, and the thought of other living beings. To do so, one should call up the thought of phenomena, thinking to oneself: 'It is simply that various phenomena have come together to form this body. It has appeared simply because phenomena appeared, and it will vanish simply because phenomena vanish. And these phenomena are none of them known to one another. When they appear, they do not say, "I have appeared!," and when they vanish, they do not say, "I have vanished!"

"Then, in order to wipe out the thought of phenomena, the ailing bodhisattva should think to himself: 'This thought or concept of phenomena too is a form of upside-down thinking, and upside-down thinking can lead to great misfortune. I must rid myself of it. But how to rid myself of it? By ridding myself of thoughts of I and mine, which means ridding myself of dualism.'

"What is meant by ridding oneself of dualism? It means not thinking of phenomena as internal or external, but treating all as equal. What is meant by equal? It means that I and nirvana are treated as equal. Why? Because I and nirvana are both empty. Why are they empty? Because they are mere names, hence empty. Neither of these two phenomena has any fixed nature or characteristics. Once one has acquired this kind of equal outlook, one will be freed of all other illness and will have only the illness of emptiness, and the illness of emptiness too is empty.

"This ailing bodhisattva of ours has no sensations of pain or pleasure, and yet he allows himself to feel such sensations, and while the Law of the Buddha is incompletely practiced he does not seek to wipe out such sensations in himself and gain entry into final enlightenment. If he feels pain in his body, he thinks of the living beings in the evil realms of existence and summons up a mind of great compassion, saying to himself: 'I have regulated and controlled myself, and now I must regulate and control other living beings!' But he should simply rid them of their illnesses and not deprive them of anything, merely teaching and guiding them so they can cut off the source of illness.

"What is meant by the source of illness? It means having troublesome entanglements. Where there are troublesome entanglements, these become the source of illness. What are these troublesome entanglements tied to? They are tied to the threefold world. And how does one cut them off? By realizing that there is nothing to grasp at. If one ceases to grasp at anything, there will be no more troublesome entanglements.

"What is meant by realizing there is nothing to grasp at? It means having done with dualistic views. What is meant by dualistic views? it means viewing this as internal, or viewing that as external. [Have done with such views] and there will be no more grasping at things.

"Manjushri, this is how the ailing bodhisattva should go about regulating and controlling his mind. By doing so, he cuts off the sufferings of old age, sickness, and death. If he fails to do so, then all his religious practice and accomplishment in the past will be void of wisdom or profit. A person who has overcome a sworn enemy deserves to be called a hero. In the same way, one who has cut off both old age, sickness, and death may be called a bodhisattva.

"This ailing bodhisattva should also think to himself: 'This illness of mine has no reality, no existence, and the illnesses of other living beings likewise have no reality and no existence.' When he adopts this view, if he should conceive a great compassion that is marked by affection and concern for living beings, he should at once thrust it aside. Why? Because the bodhisattva must rid himself of all earthly passions caused by external defilement when he summons up his great compassion. If his compassion is marked by affection and concern, then he will have feelings of weariness and revulsion toward the realm of birth and death. But if he can put aside affection and concern, he will feel no weariness and revulsion; whatever realm he happens to be born into, he will not be blinded by affection or concern.

"He is not bound by the conditions of his birth, and hence he is able to preach the Law for living beings and liberate them from their bonds. As the Buddha has said, if one is in bonds himself, to suppose he can free others from their bonds is hardly reasonable. But if one is himself free of bonds, it is perfectly reasonable to assume he can free the bonds of others. Therefore the bodhisattva must not conjure up bonds for himself.

"What is meant by bonds and what is meant by liberation? To become infatuated with the taste of meditation is the bondage of the bodhisattva. To be born in this world as a form of expedient means is the liberation of the bodhisattva. Wisdom without expedient means is bondage; wisdom with expedient means is liberation. Expedient means without wisdom is bondage; expedient means with wisdom is liberation.[2]

2. In this passage, wisdom stands for the correct mental attitude of the bodhisattva in his efforts to lead others to enlightenment, and expedient means stands for the actual methods he employs. The process of liberation or enlightenment is successfully completed only when both attitude and method are correct.

"What is meant by saying that wisdom without expedient means is bondage? It means that, with a mind full of affection and concern, a bodhisattva sets about to adorn the Buddha lands, lead numerous living beings to them, and regulate himself with the doctrines of emptiness, formlessness, and nonaction. This is called the bondage of wisdom without expedient means.

"What is meant by saying that wisdom with expedient means is liberation? It means that, with a mind free of affection and concern, a bodhisattva sets about to adorn the Buddha lands, lead numerous living beings to them, and regulate himself with the doctrines of emptiness, formlessness, and nonaction, never experiencing weariness or revulsion. This is called the liberation of wisdom with expedient means.

"What is meant by saying that expedient means without wisdom is bondage? It means that, while dwelling among the various earthly passions such as greed, anger, and erroneous views, a bodhisattva sets about planting many roots of virtue. This is called the bondage of expedient means without wisdom.

"What is meant by saying that expedient means with wisdom is liberation? It means that, while removing himself from the various earthly passions such as greed, anger, and erroneous views, a bodhisattva sets about planting many roots of virtue, bending all his efforts in the direction of anuttara-samyak-sambodhi. This is called the liberation of expedient means with wisdom.

"Manjushri, the ailing bodhisattva should view all phenomena in this way. And he should view the body and realize that it is marked by impermanence, suffering, emptiness, and absence of ego. This is called wisdom. But though his body may be ailing, he should constantly abide in the realm of birth and death, bringing benefit to all living beings and never giving in to weariness or revulsion. This is called expedient means.

"He should further view the body and realize that the body is never rid of illness, that illness is never rid of the body, and that this body and this illness are neither prior nor posterior to one another. This is called wisdom. But though his body is ailing, the bodhisattva never seeks escape into eternal extinction. This is called expedient means.

"Manjushri, the ailing bodhisattva should regulate his mind by not dwelling in such regulation, but he should not dwell in nonregulation of the mind either. Why? Because if he dwells in nonregulation of the mind, this is the way of a stupid person. But if he dwells in regulation of the mind, this is the way of a voice-hearer. Therefore the bodhisattva should dwell neither in regulation nor in nonregulation of the mind. To remove himself from such dualisms is the practice of the bodhisattva.

"To be in the realm of birth and death without following its tainted ways, to dwell in nirvana while not seeking eternal extinction—such is the practice of the bodhisattva. The practice that is neither that of common mortals nor that of worthies and sages—such is the practice of the bodhisattva. The practice that is neither sullied nor pure—such is the practice of the bodhisattva. Though far transcending the workings of devils, it shows itself in the conquering of numerous devils—such is the practice of the bodhisattva. Seeking comprehensive wisdom, yet not seeking it when the time is not right—such is the practice of the bodhisattva.

"Though he sees that all things are birthless in nature, he does not enter the realm of the absolute—such is the practice of the bodhisattva. Though he sees all in the light of the twelve-linked chain of causation, he can enter into various erroneous views—such is the practice of the bodhisattva. Though he addresses himself to all living beings, he does so without affection or attachment—such is the practice of the bodhisattva. Though he longs to be far removed from the passions, he does not seek this through elimination of the body and mind—such is the practice of the bodhisattva.

"Though he moves in the threefold world, he does no injury to the Dharma-nature—such is the practice of the bodhisattva.

Though he moves in the realm of emptiness, he plants many roots of virtue—such is the practice of the bodhisattva. Though he moves in the realm of formlessness, he yet saves many living beings—such is the practice of the bodhisattva. Though he moves in the realm of nonaction, he manifests himself by taking on a body—such is the practice of the bodhisattva. Though he avoids the arousal of passion, he rouses in himself the determination to do all good deeds—such is the practice of the bodhisattva.

"Though he practices the six paramitas, he can understand the minds and mental activities of all living beings—such is the practice of the bodhisattva. Though he is master of the six transcendental powers, he does not remove himself from all defilements—such is the practice of the bodhisattva. Though he possesses the four immeasurable qualities of mind, he is not greedy for birth in the Brahma heaven—such is the practice of the bodhisattva. Though he practices meditation, emancipation, and samadhi, he does not accept the rebirth that is consequent on these practices—such is the practice of the bodhisattva.

"Though he practices the four states of mindfulness, in the end he does not for long remove himself from the objects of such mindfulness, the body, sensations, the mind, and things—such is the practice of the bodhisattva. Though he applies himself to the four types of correct effort, he does not cease to be assiduous in matters pertaining to body and mind—such is the practice of the bodhisattva. Though he cultivates the four bases of supernatural power, he is already able to wield transcendental powers at will—such is the practice of the bodhisattva. Though he cultivates the five roots of goodness in himself, he can also distinguish whether the roots or capacities of other living beings are keen or dull—such is the practice of the bodhisattva. Though he possesses the five powers [attained through the five roots of goodness], he delights in seeking to acquire the ten powers of a Buddha—such is the practice of the bodhisattva. Though he observes the seven factors of enlightenment, he can understand all the fine points of the Buddha wisdom—such is the practice of the bodhisattva. Though he walks the eightfold holy path, he also delights in walking the immeasurable Buddha way—such is the practice of the bodhisattva.

"Though he practices concentration and insight as methods to aid one to the way, in the end he does not sink into tranquil extinction—such is the practice of the bodhisattva. Though fully aware that all things are without birth or extinction, he adorns his body with auspicious features—such is the practice of the bodhisattva. Though outwardly displaying the dignity of a voice-hearer or pratyekabuddha, he never forsakes the Buddha Law—such is the practice of the bodhisattva. Though aware that all things in the end are pure in nature, he responds to circumstances by showing himself in bodily form—such is the practice of the bodhisattva. Though insight tells him that all Buddha lands are eternally tranquil and empty in nature, yet he displays various kinds of pure Buddha lands—such is the practice of the bodhisattva. Though he attains Buddhahood, turns the wheel of the Law, and enters nirvana, in fact he never forsakes the bodhisattva way—such is the practice of the bodhisattva."

When Vimalakirti spoke these words, eight thousand heavenly sons in the great assembly led by Manjushri all set their minds on attaining anuttara-samyak-sambodhi.

*Chapter 6*

BEYOND COMPREHENSION

At that time Shariputra, observing that there were no seats in Vimalakirti's room, thought to himself: "All these bodhisattvas and major disciples—where are they going to sit?"

The rich man Vimalakirti, knowing what was in his mind, said to Shariputra, "Did you come here for the sake of the Law, or are you just looking for a place to sit?"

"I came for the Law, not for a seat!" said Shariputra.

"Ah, Shariputra," said Vimalakirti, "a seeker of the Law doesn't concern himself even about life or limb, much less about a seat! A seeker of the Law seeks nothing in the way of form, perception, conception, volition, or consciousness; he seeks nothing in the way of sense-realms or sense-media; he seeks nothing in the threefold world of desire, form, and formlessness.

"Ah, Shariputra, a seeker of the Law does not seek it through attachment to the Buddha, does not seek it through attachment to the Law, does not seek it through attachment to the order. A seeker of the Law does not seek it through recognition of suffering, does not seek it through renunciation of attachments, does not seek it through realization of how to end attachments, or through practice of the Way.[1] Why? Because the Law has nothing to do with idle theorizing. To declare that one must recognize suffering, renounce attachments, realize how to reach extinction, and practice the Way is mere idle theorizing, not seeking the Law.

75

_____

1. *These are the four noble truths, that existence is suffering, that suffering is caused by craving or attachment, that there is a way to end craving, that it can be done through practice of the eightfold path.*

"Ah, Shariputra, the Law is called 'tranquil extinction.' But if one strives for birth followed by extinction, this is seeking birth and extinction, this is not seeking the Law. The Law is called 'unstained.' But if one is stained with the idea of the Law or of nirvana, then one is stained with attachment, and this is not seeking the Law. The Law has no goal of activity, but if one actively pursues the Law, one is pursuing a goal, and this is not seeking the Law. The Law knows no picking and choosing, but if one picks and chooses the Law, this is picking and choosing, not seeking the Law. The Law is independent of place, but if one fixes on the idea of place, this is fixation with place, not a seeking of the Law. The Law is called 'formless.' If one tries to know it through form, this is seeking form, not seeking the Law.

"The Law is not something that can be resided in. If one tries to reside in it, this is trying to reside in the Law, not seeking the Law. The Law is not something that can be seen, heard, perceived, or understood. If one tries to see, hear, perceive, and understand it, this is trying to see, hear, perceive, and understand the Law, not seeking the Law. The Law is called 'unconditioned.' If one tries to approach it through the conditioned, this is seeking the conditioned, not seeking the Law.

"Therefore, Shariputra, if one would be a seeker of the Law, one must not seek it in anything at all."

76    When Vimalakirti spoke these words, five hundred heavenly sons gained the purity of the Dharma eye in their perception of phenomena.

At that time the rich man Vimalakirti said to Manjushri, "You have visited countless thousands, ten thousands, billions of asamkhyas of countries. What Buddha lands have the finest and most beautiful lion seats, those endowed with the best qualities?"

Manjushri replied, "Layman, to the east, beyond countries numerous as the sands of thirty-six Ganges, lies a world called Sumeru Shape. Its Buddha is named Sumeru Lamp King, and he is there now. This Buddha's body is eighty-four thousand yojanas in height and the lion seat [he sits on] is eighty-four thousand yojanas high and adorned in the finest fashion."

The rich man Vimalakirti then exercised his transcendental powers and at once that Buddha dispatched thirty-two thousand lion seats, tall, broad, adorned, and pure, and had them brought into Vimalakirti's room, where the bodhisattvas, major disciples, Indras, Brahmas, Four Heavenly Kings and the others saw something they had never seen before. For the room was broad and spacious enough to hold all these thirty-two thousand lion seats without the slightest crowding or hindrance. The city of Vaishali and Jambudvipa and the other of the four continents too seemed in no way cramped or inconvenienced, but all appeared just as usual.

At that time Vimalakirti said to Manjushri, "Sit down in one of the lion seats! The bodhisattvas and other distinguished persons should also sit down, but when they do so they should assume bodies suitable to the size of the seat."

The bodhisattvas who had acquired transcendental powers thereupon immediately transformed their shapes, making themselves forty-two yojanas tall, and sat down in the lion seats. But among the bodhisattvas who had newly embarked on their course or the major disciples, there were none who could climb up into the seats.

At that time Vimalakirti said to Shariputra, "Sit down in a lion seat!"

But Shariputra said, "Layman, these seats are too tall and wide—we can't climb up in them!"

Vimalakirti said, "Ah, Shariputra, if you will make obeisance to the Thus Come One Sumeru Lamp King, then you will be able to take a seat."

The bodhisattvas who had newly embarked on their course and the major disciples accordingly made obeisance to the Thus Come One Sumeru Lamp King, and after that they were able to seat themselves in the lion seats.

Shariputra said, "Layman, I have never seen such a thing! A little room like this and still it can hold seats as tall and broad as these! And the city of Vaishali is in no way crowded or obstructed, nor are any of the towns or villages of Jambudvipa or of the other of the four continents cramped or inconvenienced, or the palaces of the heavenly beings, dragon kings and spirits!"

Vimalakirti said, "Ah, Shariputra, the Buddhas and bodhisattvas have an emancipation that is called Beyond Comprehension. When a bodhisattva dwells in this emancipation, he can take something as tall and broad as Mount Sumeru and put it inside a mustard seed without enlarging one or shrinking the other, and Mount Sumeru, king of mountains, will still have its original shape. Moreover, the Four Heavenly Kings and the gods of the Trayastrimsha heaven [who live on Mount Sumeru] will not even know or realize where they have gone to. Only those destined for enlightenment will be able to see that Sumeru has been put inside a mustard seed. This is called dwelling in the doctrine of the emancipation Beyond Comprehension.

"Or again, this bodhisattva can take the waters of the four great oceans and pour them into the opening that holds a single hair, without the fish, turtles, sea turtles, lizards, or other sea creatures being in any way troubled, and those great seas will still have their original form. And the dragons, spirits, asuras, and others [who live in the sea] will not know or realize where they have gone to, and these beings will not be at all troubled.

"Or again, Shariputra, this bodhisattva who dwells in the emancipation Beyond Comprehension can slice off the thousand-millionfold world, grasp it in the palm of his right hand like a potter's wheel, and toss it beyond lands numerous as the sands of the Ganges, and the beings in that world will not know or realize where they have gotten to. The bodhisattva can then bring it back and put it in its original place, and none of the people will have any idea they have gone somewhere and come back, and the world will have the same shape as before.

"Again, Shariputra, suppose there are beings who want to live in this world for a long time but are qualified to enter enlightenment. This bodhisattva can stretch seven days into a kalpa, so that to those beings they really seem like a whole kalpa. Or if there are beings who do not want to live in this world for long and they are qualified to enter enlightenment, this bodhisattva can squeeze a kalpa into seven days, so that to those beings it seems like only seven days.

"Again, Shariputra, the bodhisattva who dwells in the emancipation Beyond Comprehension can take the magnificent adornments from all the Buddha lands, gather them together, and show them to the beings living in a single country. Or this bodhisattva can place all the beings of a single Buddha land in the palm of his right hand and fly with them all around the ten directions, showing them everything, and yet never move from his original spot.

"Or, Shariputra, this bodhisattva can take all the objects offered to the Buddhas by the beings in the worlds in the ten directions and make them all visible within a pore that holds a single hair, or take all the suns, moon, stars, and constellations that belong to the worlds in the ten directions and make them visible within the pore of a single hair. Or, Shariputra, he can suck into his mouth all the winds from the worlds in the ten directions without doing any harm to himself or breaking down the trees that grow there. Or, when the worlds in the ten directions come to the end of the kalpa and everything is destroyed by fire, he can take all those fires and hold them in his belly, and though the fires go on burning as before, the bodhisattva suffers no harm. Or he can go down into the lower region, past Buddha lands numerous as the sands of the Ganges, pick up one Buddha land, and lift it to the upper region, above Buddha lands numerous as the sands of the Ganges, as one would lift the leaf of a jujube tree on the point of a needle, and that land will be in no way troubled.

"Or, Shariputra, the bodhisattva who dwells in the emancipation Beyond Comprehension can use his transcendental powers to make himself appear in the body of a Buddha, or the body of a pratyekabuddha, or that of a voice-hearer, an Indra, a Brahma king, one of the Four Heavenly Kings, or a wheel-turning king. Or again he can take all the voices uttered by the beings in the worlds of the ten directions, high, middle, and low-grade sounds, and transform them all into the voice of the Buddha. He can make these voices discourse with the sounds of 'impermanence,' 'suffering,' 'emptiness,' or 'non-ego,' or expound all the various other doctrines preached by the Buddhas of the ten directions, and cause those doctrines to be heard everywhere.

"Shariputra, I have just now briefly described the powers possessed by this bodhisattva of the emancipation Beyond Comprehension. If I were to describe them in full, I could go on for a whole kalpa and never have done."

At that time Mahakashyapa, hearing this discourse on the doctrine of the emancipation Beyond Comprehension, sighed at encountering what he had never heard before, and said to Shariputra, "It is like someone displaying various painted images before a blind man when he cannot see them. In the same way, when we voice-hearers hear this doctrine of the emancipation Beyond Comprehension, we are all incapable of understanding it. If wise persons hear it, there will be none who do not set their minds on attaining anuttara-samyak-sambodhi. But what of us, who are forever cut off at the root, who with regard to these Great Vehicle teachings have already become like rotten seed?[2]

2. *The voice-hearers, who represent Hinayana Buddhism, because they have taken as their goal the attainment of the state of arhat, have in effect cut themselves off at the root from the search for the higher goal of Buddhahood, the goal of Great Vehicle or Mahayana Buddhist doctrine and practice. In Mahayana terms, the potential for Buddhahood inherent in the voice-hearers has become like rotten seed that will never sprout.*

When voice-hearers hear this doctrine of the emancipation Beyond Comprehension, they will surely all cry out in anguish in voices loud enough to shake the whole thousand-millionfold world. But bodhisattvas should all accept this teaching with great joy and thanksgiving. For if there are bodhisattvas who put faith in this doctrine of the emancipation Beyond Comprehension, then none of the host of devils can do anything to them!"

When Mahakashyapa spoke these words, thirty-two thousand offspring of the gods set their minds on the attainment of anuttara-samyak-sambodhi.

At that time Vimalakirti said to Mahakashyapa, "Sir, among those who play the part of devil kings in the immeasurable asamkhyas of worlds in the ten directions, there are many who in fact are bodhisattvas dwelling in the emancipation Beyond Comprehension. They employ their skill in expedient means to teach and convert living beings by appearing in the guise of devil kings.

"Or again, Kashyapa, with regard to the immeasurable numbers of bodhisattvas in the ten directions, sometimes people come to them begging for a hand or a foot, an ear, a nose, a head, an eye, marrow or brains, blood, flesh, skin, bones, or for their villages, towns, wives and children, men and women servants, elephants, horses, carriages, or for gold, lapis lazuli, seashell, agate, coral, amber, pearls, agate shell, clothing, food or drink. Many of those who beg in this fashion are bodhisattvas who dwell in the emancipation Beyond Comprehension. They employ their skill in expedient means and go to the other bodhisattvas to test them and make sure they are firm in their resolve [to give alms]. How can they do this? Because the bodhisattvas who dwell in the emancipation Beyond Comprehension possess powers of authority and virtue that enable them to importune others and make them perform difficult feats in this manner.[3] Ordinary persons of inferior type have no such powers and hence cannot importune others as these bodhisattvas do. They are like donkeys who cannot stand up before the kicking and trampling of dragons or elephants.

"This is what is called the wisdom and expedient means possessed by the bodhisattvas who dwell in the emancipation Beyond Comprehension."

3. *In speaking of people being importuned for an eye or some other part of the body, Vimalakirti probably has in mind the various tales in Buddhist lore of deities who take on devilish form and beg practitioners of the way for a piece of their body as a means of testing their dedication to the paramita of almsgiving. Vimalakirti is thus suggesting that the difficulties that Mahakashyapa and the other voice-hearers face may in fact just be a means of testing their resolve.*

*Chapter 7*

REGARDING LIVING BEINGS

At that time Manjushri asked Vimalakirti, "How does the bodhisattva regard living beings?"

Vimalakirti replied, "As a conjurer looks on the beings he conjures up—thus does the bodhisattva regard living beings. As the wise view the moon in the water, or a face or form seen in a mirror; as shimmers of heat in a torrid season, as the echo that follows a cry, as clouds in the sky, as foam on the water, bubbles on the water, as a thing no firmer that the trunk of the plantain, no longer lasting than a flash of lightning; as a fifth great element, a sixth component, a seventh sense-media, a thirteenth sense-media, a nineteenth sense-realm[1]—thus does the bodhisattva regard living beings.

"As forms in the world of formlessness, as sprouts from charred grain, as mistaken views of the body in one who has entered the stream that leads to the state of arhat, as a reentering of the womb by one no longer subject to rebirth, as the three poisons of greed, anger, and ignorance in an arhat, as greed, anger, or violation of the precepts on the part of a bodhisattva who has accepted the birthless nature of all existence, as vestiges of earthly desire in a Buddha, as forms seen by a blind person, as the breathing in and out of one immersed in the samadhi of utter tranquility, as the tracks of a bird in the sky, as a child born to a barren woman, as earthly desires in a phantom being, as sights in a dream after one has wakened, as the taking on of bodily form by one who has entered extinction, as fire that has no smoke—thus does the bodhisattva regard living beings."

83

1. *That is, as one more of each category than actually exists.*

Manjushri said, "If the bodhisattva looks on beings in this way, how can he treat them with compassion?"

Vimalakirti replied, "When the bodhisattva has finished regarding them in this way, he thinks to himself. 'For the sake of living beings I must preach this Law to them!' This is true compassion.

"He treats them with a compassion of tranquil extinction, for it results in no birth; treats them with a compassion unburning, for it is void of earthly desires; treats them with a compassion that is impartial, as the three existences of past, present, and future are impartial; treats them with a compassion free of contention, for nothing arises to oppose it; treats them with a compassion undualistic, for internal and external have no place in it; treats them with a compassion unfaltering, for it carries through to the end; treats them with a compassion firm and durable, for the mind of the bodhisattva never flags; treats them with a compassion clean and pure, as the nature of all phenomena is pure; treats them with a compassion boundless, boundless as the empty sky.

"He treats them with the compassion of the arhat, who has conquered the thieves of desire; treats them with the compassion of the bodhisattva, who brings contentment to all beings; treats them with the compassion of the Thus Come One, who has grasped the marks of Suchness; treats them with the compassion of the Buddha, who awakens living beings; treats them with a compassion wholly natural, understanding that it is causeless; treats them with a compassion of bodhi, which is of one flavor only; treats them with a compassion that has no gradation, for it cuts off all favoritism; treats them with great pity and compassion, guiding them with the Great Vehicle.

"He treats them with a compassion that never despairs, seeing that all is empty and without ego; treats them with the compassion of bestowal of the Law, never stinting in its gifts; treats them with the compassion of observance of the precepts, training those who break them to do better; treats them with the compassion of forbearance, guarding both others and self; treats them with the compassion of assiduousness, shouldering all beings as its burden; treats them with the compassion of meditation, unaffected by taste; treats them with the compassion of wisdom, which always knows the right time; treats them with the compassion of expedient means, with manifestations suited to every occasion.

"He treats them with a compassion that hides nothing, proceeding with the purity of an upright mind; treats them with the compassion of a deeply searching mind, one free of irrelevant motion; treats them with a compassion that is unerring, innocent of falsity and sham; treats them with a compassion full of peace and delight, for through it they gain the delight of the Buddha. Such is the compassion of the bodhisattva."

Continuing his questioning, Manjushri asked, "What do you mean when you speak of pity?"

"I mean that whatever benefits the bodhisattva gains, he shares them all with all other living beings," replied Vimalakirti.

Manjushri: "What do you mean by joy?"

Vimalakirti: "Any way the bodhisattva can aid or enrich others he views as an occasion for joy and never for regret."

Manjushri: "What do you mean by indifference?"

Vimalakirti: "Whatever blessings or good fortune the bodhisattva bestows, he expects nothing in return."[2]

Manjushri then asked, "If the bodhisattva fears the cycle of birth and death, what should he rely on?"

Vimalakirti replied, "The bodhisattva, fearing the cycle of birth and death, should rely on the power of the Tathagata's blessings."

Manjushri: "If he hopes to rely on the power of the Tathagata's blessings, what course should he pursue?"

2. *Compassion, pity, joy, and indifference constitute the four immeasurable qualities. See glossary.*

Vimalakirti: "If he hopes to rely on the power of the Tathagata's blessings, he should devote himself to saving and liberating all living beings."

Manjushri: "If he hopes to save living beings, what must he free them from?"

Vimalakirti: "If he hopes to save living beings, he must free them from earthly desires."

Manjushri: "If he hopes to free them from earthly desires, how should he proceed?"

Vimalakirti: "He should proceed by the method of correct mindfulness."

Manjushri: "How does one proceed by the method of correct mindfulness?"

Vimalakirti: "One proceeds on the premise of no birth and no extinction."

Manjushri: "What has no birth, and what has no extinction?"

Vimalakirti: "The not good has no birth, the good has no extinction."

Manjushri: "What is the root of good and not good?"

Vimalakirti: "The body is the root."

Manjushri: "What is the root of the body?"

Vimalakirti: "Desire and greed are the root."

Manjushri: "What is the root of desire and greed?"

86      Vimalakirti: "False and empty distinctions are the root."

Manjushri: "What is the root of false and empty distinctions?"

Vimalakirti: "Topsy-turvy thinking is the root."

Manjushri: "What is the root of topsy-turvy thinking?"

Vimalakirti: "Groundless assumptions are the root of topsy-turvy thinking."

Manjushri: "What is the root of groundless assumptions?"

Vimalakirti: "What is groundless can have no root. Manjushri, it is on the root of this groundlessness that all the other concepts are built up."

At that time there was a heavenly being, a goddess, in Vimalakirti's room who, seeing these great men and hearing them expound the Law, proceeded to make herself visible and, taking heavenly flowers, scattered them over the bodhisattvas and major disciples. When the flowers touched the bodhisattvas, they all fell to the floor at once, but when they touched the major disciples, they stuck to them and did not fall off. The disciples all tried to shake off the flowers through their supernatural powers, but they could not do so.

At that time the goddess said to Shariputra, "Why try to brush off the flowers?"

"Such flowers are not in accordance with the Law," he replied. "That's why I try to brush them off."[3]

The goddess said, "Don't say these flowers are not in accordance with the Law. Why? Because the flowers make no such distinctions. You in your thinking have made up these distinctions, that's all. If one who has left the household life to follow the Buddha's Law makes such distinctions, *that* is not in accordance with the Law. One must be without distinctions to be in accordance with the Law. Look at the bodhisattvas—the flowers do not stick to them because they have already cut off all thought of distinctions. Just as evil spirits are able to take advantage of a person who is beset by fear, so because you disciples are fearful of the cycle of birth and death, the senses of form, sound, smell, taste, and touch are able to take advantage of you. But once a person has done away with fear, then the five desires that arise from these senses will not be able to get at him. So long as one has not done away with all such entanglements, the flowers will stick to him. But they will not stick to someone who has eliminated them all."

Shariputra said, "Goddess, have you been staying in this room long?"

She replied, "Venerable sir, my stay in this room is about as long as your attainment of emancipation."

3. *The wearing of flowers or other personal ornaments was forbidden to members of the Buddhist order.*

Shariputra said, "So you've been here a long time?"

"Venerable sir," said the goddess, "how long has your attainment of emancipation been?"

Shariputra was silent and did not answer.

The goddess said, "With your great wisdom, venerable sir, why do you remain silent?"

Shariputra replied, "Emancipation cannot be spoken of in words. Therefore I do not know what I can say to you."

The goddess said, "Words, writing, all are marks of emancipation. Why? Because emancipation is not internal, not external, and not in between. And words likewise are not internal, not external, and not in between. Therefore, Shariputra, you can speak of emancipation without putting words aside. Why? Because all things that exist are marks of emancipation."

Shariputra said, "Doesn't emancipation mean putting aside lewdness, anger, and stupidity?"

The goddess said, "The Buddha, addressing persons of overbearing arrogance, asserted that one must put aside lewdness, anger, and stupidity in order to gain emancipation, that is all. If he was addressing those who were free of overbearing arrogance, the Buddha asserted that the nature of lewdness, anger, and stupidity is emancipation itself."

Shariputra said, "Excellent, excellent! Goddess, what have you seized on, what have you seen into, that you speak with such eloquence?"

The goddess replied, "I have seized on nothing, seen into nothing, and hence speak with eloquence. Why? If one claims to have seized on something or seen into something, then in the light of the Buddha's Law one is being overbearingly arrogant."

Shariputra asked the goddess, "Of the three vehicles, which do you pursue?"

The goddess replied, "I use the Law of the voice-hearer to convert living beings, and therefore I practice the way of the voice-hearer. I use the Law of causes and conditions to convert

The goddess said, "All things are just the same—they have no fixed form. So why ask why I don't change out of my female form?"

At that time the goddess employed her supernatural powers to change Shariputra into a goddess like herself, while she took on Shariputra's form. Then she asked, "Why don't you change out of this female body?"

Shariputra, now in the form of a goddess, replied, "I don't know why I have suddenly changed and taken on a female body!"

The goddess said, "Shariputra, if you can change out of this female body, then all women can change likewise. Shariputra, who is not a woman, appears in a woman's body. And the same is true of all women—though they appear in women's bodies, they are not women. Therefore the Buddha teaches that all phenomena are neither male nor female."

Then the goddess withdrew her supernatural powers, and Shariputra returned to his original form. The goddess said to Shariputra, "Where now is the form and shape of your female body?"

Shariputra said, "The form and shape of my female body does not exist, yet does not not exist."

The goddess said, "All things are just like that—they do not exist, yet do not not exist. And that they do not exist, yet do not not exist, is exactly what the Buddha teaches."

Shariputra said to the goddess, "When your present existence comes to an end, where will you be reborn?"

The goddess replied, "The way the Buddha is born in his transformation body—that's how I'll be born."[5]

Shariputra said, "When the Buddha is born in his transformation body, it is not a matter of birth or death.

---

5. *The Buddha takes on a "transformation body" when he appears in one of the lower realms of existence in order to guide and instruct the beings there. See glossary, under "three bodies."*

The goddess said, "It's that way with living beings too—they are without birth or death."

Shariputra said to the goddess, "How long will it be before you attain anuttara-samyak-sambodhi?"

The goddess replied, "Shariputra, when you revert to the state of a common unenlightened mortal, then I will succeed in gaining anuttara-samyak-sambodhi."

Shariputra said, "It is unthinkable that I should become a common mortal again!"

The goddess said, "It is likewise unthinkable that I should attain anuttara-samyak-sambodhi. Why? Because bodhi is nothing to be thought about, hence nothing to be attained."

Shariputra said, "The Buddhas who are now attaining anuttara-samyak-sambodhi, and those who have attained it in the past and will attain it in the future, numerous as the sands of the Ganges—what would you say of all those?"

The goddess said, "We use the numbers of everyday language, and so we speak of all those as belonging to the three existences of past, present, and future. But this is not to say that bodhi knows anything of past, present, and future."

Then the goddess said, "Shariputra, have you attained the way of the arhat?"

Shariputra said, "I've realized there is nothing to be attained, so I've attained it."

The goddess said, "The Buddhas and bodhisattvas are that way too. They've realized there is nothing to attain, and so they've attained it."

At this time Vimalakirti said to Shariputra, "This goddess has in the past made offerings to ninety-two million Buddhas and can disport herself with the supernatural powers of a bodhisattva. She has fulfilled all that she vowed, has accepted the truth of birthlessness, and dwells in a state from which she will never regress. Because of her original vow, she can show herself anytime she wishes and teach and convert living beings."

*Chapter 8*

At that time Manjushri asked Vimalakirti, "How does the bodhisattva go about mastering the Buddha way?"

Vimalakirti said, "The bodhisattva should follow a path that is not the way—then he can master the Buddha way."

Manjushri asked, "How does the bodhisattva follow a path that is not the way?"

Vimalakirti replied, "If the bodhisattva goes to the region of the five sins that lead to the hell of incessant suffering, he shows no anguish or anger. He arrives in hell, but is free of offense or defilement. He arrives in the realm of beasts, but without the faults of stupidity or arrogance. He arrives in the realm of the hungry spirits, yet is fully endowed with merits. He goes to the world of form and the world of formlessness, but makes no boast of this.

"He shows greed and desire in his actions, yet is removed from the stains of attachment. He shows anger in his actions, yet has no anger or aversion toward living beings. He appears to be stupid, but utilizes wisdom to regulate his mind. He appears stingy and grasping, yet relinquishes both inner and outer possessions, begrudging neither body nor life. He appears to break the commandments, but in fact resides secure in the pure precepts, and even then remains fearful of committing the smallest fault.

"He seems angry and irascible, yet is at all times compassionate and forbearing. He seems indolent and lazy, yet works diligently to acquire merit. He seems disordered in thought, yet constantly practices meditation. He seems stupid, yet has mastered both worldly and otherworldly wisdom.

93

"He appears fawning and deceitful, but is skilled in expedient means and faithful to the sutra doctrines. He appears haughty and arrogant, yet serves as a bridge and a crossing for living beings. He appears to be immersed in earthly desires, but his mind is at all times clear and pure.

"We see him going among devils, yet he abides by the Buddha wisdom and heeds no other teachings. We see him going among voice-hearers, but to living beings he preaches a Law never heard before. We see him going among pratyekabuddhas, but he manifests great pity in teaching and converting living beings.

"He seems to be among the poor and destitute, yet he has jeweled hands capable of bestowing inexhaustible benefits. He seems to be crippled and deformed, yet possesses auspicious features, adorning himself wonderfully with them. He seems to be humble and lowly, yet is born into the seed and lineage of the Buddha, fully endowed with blessings. He seems to be among the puny and emaciated, the ugly and vile, yet acquires the body of a Narayana, a delight for all beings to see.[1] He seems to be old and ailing, yet has forever cut off the roots of illness and transcended the fear of death.

"He appears to possess wealth, but habitually regards it as transient and in fact covets none of it. He seems to have wives, concubines, and waiting women, yet never sullies himself in the bog of the five desires. He seems thick-tongued and clumsy in speech, yet commands great eloquence and retains all he has learned, forgetting nothing. Though appearing to employ unorthodox methods of salvation, he follows the correct teaching in saving living beings. He appears to enter all the different paths of existence, yet cuts himself off from their influence. He appears to have entered nirvana, yet never cuts himself off from the realm of birth and death.

94

1. *Narayana, an incarnation of Vishnu, is incorporated into Buddhism as a guardian deity noted for his heroic strength and stature.*

"Manjushri, by going to places that are the opposite of the way in this fashion, the bodhisattva is able to master the Buddha way."

Vimalakirti than asked Manjushri, "What may act as the seeds of the Thus Come One?"[2]

Manjushri said, "The body is the seed, ignorance and partiality are the seeds, greed, anger, and stupidity are the seeds. The four topsy-turvy views are the seeds, the five obscurations are the seeds, the six sense-media are the seeds, the seven abodes of consciousness are the seeds, the eight errors are the seeds, the nine sources of anxiety are the seeds, the ten evil actions are the seeds. To sum it up, the sixty-two erroneous views and all the different kinds of earthly desires are all the seeds of the Buddha."

"What do you mean by that?"

Manjushri replied, "A person who has perceived the uncreated nature of reality and entered into correct understanding cannot again set his mind on attaining anuttara-samyak-sambodhi. The lotus does not grow on the upland plain; the lotus grows in the mud and mire of a damp low-lying place. In the same way, the Buddha Law can never grow in a person who has perceived the uncreated nature of reality and entered into correct understanding. It is only when living beings are in the midst of the mire of earthly desires that they turn to the Buddha Law.

"If you plant seeds in the sky, they will never grow. Only when you plant them in well-manured soil can they sprout and flourish. In the same way, the Buddha Law will never grow in a person who has perceived the uncreated nature of reality and entered into correct understanding. But one who entertains egoistic views as huge as Mount Sumeru can still set his mind on the attainment of anuttara-samyak-sambodhi. From this you should understand that all the various earthly desires are the seeds of the Thus Come One. If you do not descend into the vast

95

---

2. *That is, the seeds leading to enlightenment or Buddhahood.*

ocean, you can never acquire a priceless pearl. In the same way, if you do not enter the great sea of earthly desires, you can never acquire the treasure of comprehensive wisdom."

At that time Mahakashyapa sighed and said, "Excellent, excellent, Manjushri! These words are aptly spoken. It is indeed just as you say. Those who are troubled by the passions are the seeds of the Thus Come One. But persons such as us, [the voice-hearers], are now no longer capable of setting our minds on the attainment of anuttara-samyak-sambodhi. Even those who have committed the five sins that lead to the hell of incessant suffering can still rouse aspirations that will afford growth to the Buddha Law. But now we can never rouse such aspirations. We are like persons whose faculties are impaired and can no longer satisfy the five desires. The voice-hearers, who have cut off all entanglements, are like this, for they can no longer bene-fit from the Buddha Law, nor will they ever have the desire to.

"In this sense, Manjushri, the common mortal responds with gratitude to the Buddha Law but the voice-hearer does not. Why do I say this? Because when the common mortal hears the Buddha Law, he can set his mind on attaining the unsurpassed way, determined that the Three Treasures shall never perish. But the voice-hearer may hear of the Buddha's Law and powers and fearlessness to the end of his life and yet never be capable of rousing in himself an aspiration for the unsurpassed way."

At that time there was in the assembly a bodhisattva named Universally Manifested Physical Body who asked Vimalakirti, "Layman, your father and mother, wife and children, relatives, retainers, clerks, people, and friends—who are they? Your maids and men servants, your elephants, horses, and carriages—where are they?"

Vimalakirti replied with the following verses:

> Wisdom is the bodhisattva's mother,
> expedient means his father;

of those who guide and teach all beings,
there are none not born of these.

Dharma joy is his wife,
pity and compassion of mind are his
    daughters,
the good mind and sincerity his sons,
final emptiness and tranquility his dwelling.

For disciples he has the many dusts and
    passions;
they follow the dictates of his will.
The thirty-seven elements of the Way are his
    good friends;
through them he gains correct enlightenment.

The paramitas are his Dharma companions,
the four methods of winning others, his
    singing girls.
For songs they carol the words of the Dharma;
such is the music made for him.

In the garden of full retention of the
    teachings
grow the trees of the Law free of outflows.
Their wonderful blossoms are the seven
    factors of enlightenment,
their fruit, emancipation and wisdom.

On the bathing-pool of the eight
    emancipations,
brimming with clear waters of meditation,
spread the lotuses of the seven purities;
those who bathe there are spotless.

His elephants and horses race the five roads of
    transcendental power,
for chariot he has the Great Vehicle.
Controling, directing with the single mind,
he travels the eightfold path.

His form displays all the auspicious marks,
every good feature adorns him.
He is clothed in the garments of shame and
    remorse,
a deeply searching mind his garland.

For wealth he has the treasure of the seven
    assets
which he teaches to others, enriching them.
He practices as the teachings direct,
his great profits he shares with others.

His couch is the four meditations,
where the pure way of life is born.
He hears much, augmenting his
    wisdom,
sounding the call of self-awakening.

The sweet dew of the Law is his food,
sauced with the flavor of emancipation.
He bathes in purification of the mind,
anointing himself with the perfume of the
    precepts.

He wipes out the thieves of earthly desire;
his valor cannot be outshone.
He conquers and subdues the four kinds of
    devils,

his victory banners fly over the place of
   practice.

Though he knows there is no arising or
   extinction,
he undergoes birth so he may instruct others.
In every land he manifests himself;
like the sun, nowhere is he not seen.

To the countless millions of Thus Come Ones
of the ten directions he gives alms,
yet he never thinks of these Buddhas
as in any way separate from himself.

Though he knows that the Buddha lands,
along with living beings, are empty,
yet constantly he works to purify the lands,
teaching and converting the many beings.

The form and voice and behavior
of every manner of living being—
the bodhisattva with his fearless powers
can take on any of these in an instant.

99

He understands all devilish affairs
and can imitate the actions of devils.
Wise in the skillful use of expedient means,
he can manifest all such forms at will.

At times he shows himself old, sick, dying,
in order to waken living beings,
so they will realize they are like conjured
   phantoms
and gain understanding free of all obstacles.

Sometimes he shows the kalpa ending in
    flames,
heaven and earth consumed with all else,
so that people who think of things as
    permanent
will clearly perceive their impermanence.

Countless billions of living beings
come in company to visit the bodhisattva,
all arriving at his house at the same moment;
he converts them, directs them to the Buddha
    way.

Secular writings, secret spells and
    incantations,
crafts, skills, the many arts—
all these he shows himself adept in,
so he may aid and benefit living beings.

He becomes a monk
in all the different creeds of the world
so that thereby he may free others from
    delusion
and save them from falling into erroneous
    beliefs.

At times he becomes the sun, the moon, a
    heavenly being,
an Indra, a Brahma, lord of the world;
at others he may become earth or water,
or again become wind or fire.

If during the kalpa there is pestilence,
he manifests himself as medicinal herbs;

those who drink potions made from them
will be healed of sickness, cleansed of all
    poison.

If during the kalpa there is famine,
he manifests his body as food and drink,
first relieving hunger and thirst,
then telling people of the Law.

If during the kalpa there is a clash of arms,
he accordingly rouses a mind of compassion,
converting those living beings,
causing them to dwell in a land without
    contention.

When great armies confront each other in
    the field,
he causes them to be of equal might,
manifesting his bodhisattva power and
    authority,
subduing them and restoring peace.

In whatever country
hells exist,
at once he sets out, journeys there,
striving to relieve their sufferings.

In whatever country
beasts are devouring one another,
in all his births he manifests himself there
so he can bring aid to those lands.

He shows himself subject to the five desires
yet is also seen to practice meditation,

causing the devils' minds to be dazed and
    confounded
so they cannot take advantage of others.

To live as a lotus among flames—
this may be deemed a rare thing.
To exist amid desire yet practice meditation—
this too is rare!

Sometimes he shows himself as a woman of
    pleasure,
enticing those prone to lechery.
First he catches them with the hook of desire,
then leads them into the Buddha way.

Sometimes he appears as a village headman,
other times as leader of the merchants,
as a teacher of the nation, a high-placed official,
abetting and profiting all beings.

Where there are those in poverty and want
he shows himself with limitless stores,
using them to encourage and lead others,
causing them to set their minds on attaining
    bodhi.

Among those arrogant and full of ego
he becomes a man of great strength,
overpowering and curbing their haughtiness,
causing them to dwell in the unsurpassed way.

Where there are those timid and quailing
he stands at their head to lend assurance.
First he fills them with fearlessness,
then causes them to set their minds on the way.

Sometimes he is seen renouncing lust and
    desire
to become a holy man of the five transcenden-
    tal powers,
opening the way, guiding living beings,
causing them to dwell in the precepts, forbear-
    ance and compassion.

If there are those looking for servants,
he shows himself as a groom or menial,
and after delighting his employers,
he rouses in them a mind for the way.

Whatever others are looking for,
he supplies it to win them to the Buddha way.
With his skill in the power of expedient means
he can satisfy all their wants.

Thus his ways are beyond measure,
his practices know no bounds;
infinite in wisdom,
he saves and emancipates countless beings.

Though all the Buddhas
for numberless billions of kalpas
should praise the merits he achieves,
they could never finish doing so.

Who can hear of this Law
and not set his mind on the attainment of
    bodhi?
Who but the utterly worthless,
the blindly ignorant, the witless?

## Chapter 9

ENTERING THE GATE OF NONDUALISM

At that time Vimalakirti said to the various bodhisattvas, "Sirs, how does the bodhisattva go about entering the gate of nondualism? Let each one explain as he understands it."

One of the bodhisattvas in the assembly, whose name was Dharma Freedom, spoke these words: "Sirs, birth and extinction form a dualism. But since all dharmas are not born to begin with, they must now be without extinction. By grasping and learning to accept this truth of birthlessness, one may enter the gate of nondualism."

The bodhisattva Virtue Guardian said, " 'I' and 'mine' form a dualism. Because there is an 'I', there is also a 'mine.' But if there is no 'I,' there will be no 'mine.' In this way one enters the gate of nondualism."

The bodhisattva Unblinking said, "Perception and nonperception form a dualism. But if dharmas are not perceived, then there is nothing to take hold of. And because there is nothing to take hold of, there will be no grasping, no rejecting, no action, no volition. In this way one enters the gate of nondualism."

The bodhisattva Virtue Peak said, "Defilement and purity form a dualism. But if one sees into the true nature of defilement, it is without the marks of purity but leads into the extinction of all marks. In this way one enters the gate of nondualism."

The bodhisattva Good Constellation said, "The stirring of the mind and thought—these two form a dualism. But if the mind is not stirred, then there will be no thought. And if there is no thought, there will be no discrimination. The one who has thoroughly mastered this may in this way enter the gate of nondualism."

The bodhisattva Good Eye said, "The unique in form and the formless constitute a dualism. But if one understands that the unique in form is in fact the formless, and then does not seize on the formless but sees all as equal, one may in this way enter the gate of nondualism."

The bodhisattva Wonderful Arm said, "The bodhisattva mind and the voice-hearer mind constitute a dualism. But if one regards the mind as empty in form, like a conjured phantom, then there is no bodhisattva mind and no voice-hearer mind. In this way one may enter the gate of nondualism."

The bodhisattva Pushya[1] said, "Good and not good form a dualism. But if one does not call up either good or not good but enters into the realm of the formless and truly masters it, in this way one may enter the gate of nondualism."

The bodhisattva Lion said, "Blame and blessing form a dualism. But if one penetrates the true nature of blame, it is no different from blessing. When one can dispose of forms with this diamondlike wisdom, neither bound nor liberated, one may in this way enter the gate of nondualism."

The bodhisattva Lion Will said, "Presence of outflows of passion and absence of such outflows constitute a dualism. But if one can grasp the fact that all dharmas are equal, then one will not give rise to the concept of outflows or no outflows. One will not be attached to form nor dwell in formlessness either. In this way one may enter the gate of nondualism."

The bodhisattva Pure Understanding said, "The created and the uncreated form a dualism. But if one does away with all enumerations, then the mind is like empty sky, freed of all obstacles through pure clean wisdom. In this way one enters the gate of nondualism."

---

1. Pushya (Puṣya) is the twenty-third of the twenty-eight constellations or stellar mansions of Indian astrology, the constellation under whose influence this bodhisattva was born.

The bodhisattva Narayana said, "The worldly and the unworldly form a dualism. But since the nature of the worldly is empty, the worldly is in fact the unworldly. Neither entering into it nor going out of it, neither exceeding nor falling short—in this way one enters the gate of nondualism."

The bodhisattva Good Will said, "The realm of birth and death and that of nirvana form a dualism. But if one sees the true nature of birth and death, one sees that there is no birth or death, no binding, no unbinding, no birth,[2] no extinction. One who understands in this way may thereby enter the gate of nondualism."

The bodhisattva Direct Seeing said, "The exhaustible and the inexhaustible form a dualism. But whether dharmas are in the end exhaustible or inexhaustible, they are all without the marks of exhaustibility. And if they are without the marks of exhaustibility, they are empty. And if they are empty, they are without the marks either of exhaustibility or inexhaustibility. If one enters this realm of understanding, one my thereby enter the gate of nondualism."

The bodhisattva Universal Guardian said, " 'I' and 'not-I' form a dualism. But when one cannot grasp even 'I,' how can one grasp 'not-I'? One who has seen into the true nature of 'I' will no longer give rise to these two concepts, and in this way enter the gate of nondualism."

106    The bodhisattva Lightning God said, "Enlightenment and ignorance form a dualism. But the true nature of ignorance is none other than enlightenment. And enlightenment cannot be seized, but is apart from all enumerations. One dwells in the center, in the equality without dualism, and in this way enters the gate of nondualism."

The bodhisattva Joyful Seeing said, "Form and the emptiness of form constitute a dualism. But form is none other than

2. *In place of* sheng, *"birth," some texts read* jan, *"burning;" that is, no burning of the fire of passion, no putting out of the fire.*

emptiness; emptiness does not represent the extinction of form. Form is itself empty by nature. In the same way perception, conception, volition, and consciousness, and the emptiness of consciousness, constitute dualisms. But consciousness is none other than emptiness; emptiness does not represent the extinction of consciousness. Consciousness is itself empty by nature.[3] Dwelling in the midst of these concepts and understanding them thoroughly, one may in this way enter the gate of nondualism."

The bodhisattva Enlightened as to Form said, "To regard the four elements [earth, water, fire, and wind] as different from the element emptiness or space is dualistic. The nature of the four elements is none other than the nature of emptiness. Just as the past and future of these elements is empty, so too must their present be empty. If one can understand the nature of the elements in this way, one may thereby enter the gate of nondualism."

The bodhisattva Wonderful Will said, "The eye and the objects it observes constitute a dualism. But if one understands the nature of the eye, then with regard to objects one will be without greed, without anger, and without stupidity. This is called tranquil extinction. Similarly, the ear and sounds, the nose and smells, the tongue and tastes, the body and touch, and the mind and phenomena constitute dualisms. But if one understands the nature of the mind, then with regard to phenomena one will be without greed, without anger, and without stupidity. This is called tranquil extinction. Dwelling at rest in its midst, one may thereby enter the gate of nondualism."

---

3. *The text spells out the argument in full only in the case of the first and last terms in the series, form and consciousness, but the same argument applies to the other terms, perception, conception, and volition. This same type of abbreviated construction is used in the next answer and in several of those that follow.*

The bodhisattva Inexhaustible Will said, "Almsgiving, and applying the merits gained thereby to acquire comprehensive wisdom, constitute a dualism. But the nature of almsgiving is none other than the applying of merits to acquire comprehensive wisdom. Similarly, keeping of the precepts, forbearance, assiduousness, meditation, and wisdom form dualisms in contrast to the applying of merit to acquire comprehensive wisdom, etc. But the nature of wisdom is none other than the applying of merits to acquire comprehensive wisdom. By entering into an understanding of the singleness of form that all these share, one may thus enter the gate of nondualism."

The bodhisattva Deep Wisdom said, "This is emptiness, this is formlessness, this is nonaction—to speak in this manner is dualistic. Emptiness is none other than formlessness, formlessness is none other than nonaction. If something is empty, formless, nonacting, then it is without mind, will, or consciousness. This single doctrine of emancipation is the same as the threefold doctrine of emancipation [regarding emptiness, formlessness, and nonaction]. In this way one enters the gate of nondualism."

The bodhisattva Tranquil Roots said, "To speak of the Buddha, the Law, and the assembly is dualistic. The Buddha is none other than the Law, the Law is none other than the assembly. These Three Treasures are all uncreated in form, like the empty sky, and all dharmas are the same. One who can act in accordance with this understanding may thereby enter the gate of nondualism."

The bodhisattva Mind Unobstructed said, "The body and the body extinguished constitute a dualism. But the body is none other than the body extinguished. Why? Because one who sees into the true form of the body does not give rise to thoughts of seeing the body or seeing the extinction of the body. The body and the extinction of the body are not two things, not a distinction to be made. One who rests in this understanding, neither alarmed nor fearful, may in this way enter the gate of nondualism."

The bodhisattva Superior Goodness said, "To speak of the activities of body, mouth, and mind is dualistic. These three activities are all marked by the aspect of nonaction. If the body is marked by nonaction, then the mouth must be marked by nonaction, and if the mouth is marked by nonaction, then the mind must be marked by nonaction. And since these three activities are marked by nonaction, then all dharmas must be marked by nonaction. One who can go along with this wisdom of nonaction may in this way enter the gate of nondualism."

The bodhisattva Merit Field said, "To speak of meritorious deeds, blameful deeds, and deeds that call forth no retribution is dualistic. The true nature of all three kinds of deeds is empty. And if it is empty, then there are no meritorious deeds, no blameful deeds, and no deeds that call forth no retribution. One who does not rouse any thought of distinctions with regard to these three types of deeds may thereby enter the gate of nondualism."

The bodhisattva Flower Garland said, "From the concept of 'self' rises the concept of two things, [self and other,] which creates a dualism. But one who sees into the true form of the self will not give rise to the thought of two things. [And if one does not dwell in the thought of two things, then one will be without consciousness and without anything one is conscious of, and in this way may enter the gate of nondualism."]

The bodhisattva Virtue Storehouse said, "To suppose that there is some form or object that one can acquire is dualistic. But if one realizes that there is nothing to be acquired, then there will be no grasping and no rejecting. And when there is no grasping and no rejecting, one may in this way enter the gate of nondualism."

The bodhisattva Moon in Midair said, "Darkness and light form a dualism; if there is no darkness and no light, there will be no dualism. Why? It is like entering the meditation that wipes out perception and conception, where there is neither darkness nor light. And the forms of all dharmas are the same as this. If one enters this state and views all with equality, one may thereby enter the gate of nondualism."

The bodhisattva Treasure Sign said, "To yearn for nirvana and not delight in the world constitutes a dualism. But if one does not yearn for nirvana and does not loathe the world, there will be no dualism. Why? If there is binding, there will be unbinding. But if there is no binding to begin with, who will seek to be unbound? And where there is no binding and unbinding, there will be no yearning and no loathing, and in this way one may enter the gate of nondualism."

The bodhisattva Jewel Crowned King said, "The correct way and the erroneous way constitute a dualism. But one who dwells in the correct way does not make distinctions, saying 'This is erroneous!' or 'This is correct!' By removing oneself from both, one may thereby enter the gate of nondualism."

The bodhisattva Delight in Truth said, "The true and the not true form a dualism. But one who sees truly cannot even see the true, so how can he see the untrue? Why? Because they cannot be seen by the physical eye; only the eye of wisdom can see them. But for this eye of wisdom there is no seeing and no not seeing. In this way one may enter the gate of nondualism."

110 When the various bodhisattvas had finished one by one giving their explanations, they asked Manjushri, "How then does the bodhisattva enter the gate of nondualism?"

Manjushri replied, "To my way of thinking, all dharmas are without words, without explanations, without purport, without cognition, removed from all questions and answers. In this way one may enter the gate of nondualism."

Then Manjushri said to Vimalakirti, "Each of us has given an explanation. Now, sir, it is your turn to speak. How does the bodhisattva enter the gate of nondualism?"

At that time Vimalakirti remained silent and did not speak a word.

Manjushri sighed and said, "Excellent, excellent! Not a word, not a syllable—this truly is to enter the gate of nondualism!"

When this chapter on Entering the Gate of Nondualism was preached, five thousand bodhisattvas in the assembly were all able to enter the gate of nondualism and to learn to accept the truth of birthlessness.

## Chapter 10

FRAGRANCE ACCUMULATED

At that time Shariputra thought to himself, "It is almost noon. What are all these bodhisattvas going to eat?"

Then Vimalakirti, knowing what was in his mind, said, "The Buddha preached the eight emancipations. You, sir, should undertake to practice them. Why be distracted by thoughts of eating when you are listening to the Law? If you want something to eat, wait a moment. I will see that you get the sort of food you have never had before!"

Vimalakirti then entered samadhi and, employing his transcendental powers, showed the great assembly a country called Many Fragrances, situated in a region high above, beyond Buddha lands as numerous as the sands of forty-two Ganges. The Buddha named Fragrance Accumulated was at that time present there. The fragrance of his country was finer than the fragrance of all the human and heavenly realms of the Buddha lands of the ten directions. In his land there was not even the term voice-hearer or pratyekabuddha, but only great bodhisattvas, pure and clean, for whom the Buddha preached the Law. All the inhabitants of his world built their halls and towers out of fragrances, strolled the fragrant ground, and had gardens all made of fragrances. The fragrant aroma of their food wafted to immeasurable worlds in the ten directions. At this time the Buddha and the various bodhisattvas were just sitting down together to eat. Heavenly offspring, all named Fragrant Garland, all with their minds set on attaining anuttara-samyak-sambodhi, were serving the meal to the Buddha and the bodhisattvas.

Among the great assembly [gathered at Vimalakirti's house,] there were none who could not see these things with their own eyes.

Then Vimalakirti addressed the bodhisattvas, saying, "Sirs, who among you can bring us some of that Buddha's food?"

Out of deference to Manjushri's authority and supernatural powers, however, all of them remained silent.

[Addressing Manjushri,] Vimalakirti said, "Sir, a great assembly such as this—this is shameful, is it not?"

Manjushri replied, "As the Buddha has told us, never despise those who have yet to learn."

Thereupon Vimalakirti, without rising from his seat but in the presence of the whole gathering, conjured up a phantom bodhisattva whose auspicious features, shining brightness, authority and virtue were so superior that they outshone the entire group. Then he announced to this bodhisattva, "You must go to the region high above, beyond Buddha lands numerous as the sands of forty-two Ganges, where there is a country called Many Fragrances. The Buddha, named Fragrance Accumulated, is just now sitting down with his bodhisattvas to a meal. When you arrive in his presence, speak as I instruct you, saying, 'Vimalakirti bows his head before the feet of the World-Honored One with immeasurable reverence and begs to inquire if in your daily activities your illnesses are few, your worries are few. Does your strength suffice you? He desires to obtain the leftovers from this meal of the World-Honored One so he may carry out the Buddha's work by dispensing them in the saha world, enabling those who delight in a lesser doctrine to be broadened by the great way, and also to cause the Thus Come One's fame to be heard on all sides.' "

At that time this conjured bodhisattva in the presence of the gathering ascended to the region high above. Everyone in the entire assembly could see him as he departed, and as he arrived in the world called Many Fragrances and made his obeisance at the feet of the Buddha there. And they could hear him say, 'Vimalakirti bows his head before the feet of the World-Honored One with immeasurable reverence and begs to inquire if in your daily activities your illnesses are few, your worries are few. Does your strength suffice you? He desires to obtain the leftovers from this meal of the World-Honored One so he may carry out the Buddha's work by dispensing them in the saha world, ensuring that those who delight in a lesser doctrine will be broadened by the great way, and also that the Thus Come One's fame may be heard on all sides."

When the great men [of the country Many Fragrances] saw this conjured bodhisattva, they sighed at seeing what they had never seen before, and said, "Where has this superior being come from? The saha world—where is that? What is this thing he calls a 'lesser doctrine?' "[1]

When they had put these questions to their Buddha, the Buddha announced to them, "In the lower region, beyond Buddha lands as numerous as the sands of forty-two Ganges, there is a world called saha. The Buddha named Shakyamuni is at present manifesting himself in that evil world of the five impurities in order to expound the teachings of the Way to living beings who delight in a lesser doctrine. He has a bodhisattva named Vimalakirti who dwells in the emancipation Beyond Comprehension and preaches the Law for the other bodhisattvas. He has purposely dispatched this phantom being to come and extol my name and praise this land, so that thereby he may bring increased benefits to those bodhisattvas."

The bodhisattvas said, "How can this man conjure up a phantom such as this? Does he possess such strength of virtue, such fearlessness, such transcendental powers?"

---

1. *The inhabitants of the country Many Fragrances, as we have been told earlier, have never even heard of voice-hearers or pratyekabuddhas.*

The Buddha replied, "His powers are great indeed! He dispatches phantoms in all the ten directions to carry out the Buddha's work and bring enrichment to living beings."

Then the Thus Come One Fragrance Accumulated took a bowl of many fragrances, filled it with fragrant rice, and gave it to the phantom bodhisattva.

At that time the nine million bodhisattvas all spoke out in unison, saying, "We wish to visit that saha world and offer alms to Shakyamuni Buddha. And we also wish to see Vimalakirti and the many other bodhisattvas."

"You may go," said the Buddha. "But draw in your bodily fragrances so that you will not cause living beings to be deluded or beguiled by them. And you should put aside your real form so that the persons in that country who are striving to become bodhisattvas will not feel intimidated or ashamed. And you must not look on that land with disdain or contempt or rouse thoughts that obstruct progress. Why? Because all the lands in the ten directions are as empty as the sky. It is just that, since the Buddhas wish to convert those who delight in a lesser doctrine, they do not reveal the full purity of the land."

At that time the phantom bodhisattva, having received the bowl of rice, joined the nine million bodhisattvas and all, relying upon the might and supernatural power of the Buddha and upon Vimalakirti's power, suddenly vanished from that world and then in the space of an instant arrived at Vimalakirti's house.

Vimalakirti immediately conjured up nine million lion seats, beautifully adorned like the ones that were already there, and the bodhisattvas all sat down in them.

The bodhisattva then presented the bowl filled with fragrant rice to Vimalakirti. The fragrance of the rice perfumed the entire city of Vaishali and the whole thousand-millionfold world. The Brahmans, lay believers, and others of Vaishali, smelling this fragrant aroma, were delighted in body and mind, sighing with admiration at something they had never known before.

At that time Moon Canopy, a leader among the rich men, accompanied by eighty-four thousand persons, came to Vimalakirti's house. Seeing the vast number of bodhisattvas gathered in the room and the lion seats, tall, broad, and beautifully adorned, they were all filled with delight. After paying obeisance to the bodhisattvas and the major disciples, they retired and stood to one side. Various earth deities, sky deities, and heavenly beings of the world of desire and the world of form, smelling the fragrant aroma, all likewise came to Vimalakirti's house.

Then Vimalakirti said to Shariputra and the other great voice-hearers, "Sirs, come eat this rice from the Thus Come One, delicious as sweet dew. It is redolent with the odor of great pity. But you must not eat it in a narrow-minded manner, or you will never digest it!"

Some of the other voice-hearers thought to themselves, "There is only a little rice—how can it feed all the people in this great assembly?"

But the phantom bodhisattva said, "Do not try to use your voice-hearers' petty virtue and petty wisdom in appraising the immeasurable blessings and wisdom of the Thus Come One! Though the four seas run dry, this rice will never come to an end. Every person here could eat helpings the size of Mount Sumeru, and do so for a whole kalpa, but still it would never be exhausted. Why? Because this is the leftovers from a meal eaten by persons who have acquired inexhaustible merits through the precepts, meditation, wisdom, emancipation, and the insight of emancipation. Therefore it can never be exhausted."

The rice in the bowl was then used to feed to satisfaction all the members of the assembly, yet it remained as it was, without any sign of depletion. The bodhisattvas, voice-hearers, and heavenly and human beings who ate the rice had a sense of bodily ease and delight of mind, like the bodhisattvas in the Country of All Delights and Adornments. And a wonderful fragrance emanated from the pores of all of them, like the fragrance of the trees in the land called Many Fragrances.

At that time Vimalakirti asked the bodhisattvas from the country Many Fragrances, "How does the Thus Come One Fragrance Accumulated preach the Law?"

The bodhisattvas replied, "The Thus Come One in our land does not employ words in his exposition. He just uses various fragrances to induce heavenly and human beings to undertake the observance of the precepts. Each bodhisattva sits under a fragrant tree, and when he smells the marvelous fragrance, he immediately attains the samadhi known as the Storehouse of All Virtues. Persons who are able to attain this samadhi all become endowed with the blessings of a bodhisattva."

The bodhisattvas then asked Vimalakirti, "Now how does the World-Honored One Shakyamuni preach the Law?"

Vimalakirti replied, "The living beings of this land are stubborn and strong-willed and hard to convert. Therefore the Buddha uses strong language when preaching to them in order to tame and control them. He says, 'This is hell, this is the realm of beasts, this is the realm of hungry spirits, these are the difficult conditions, this is the place where stupid people are born. These are misdeeds of the body, these are the retribution for misdeeds of the body. These are misdeeds of the mouth, these are the retribution for misdeeds of the mouth. These are misdeeds of the mind, these are the retribution for misdeeds of the mind.

" 'This is the killing of living beings, this is the retribution for killing living beings. This is taking what has not been given to you, this is the retribution for taking what has not been given to you. This is sexual misconduct, this is the retribution for sexual misconduct. This is lying, this is the retribution for lying. This is being double-tongued, this is the retribution for being double-tongued. This is harsh speech, this is the retribution for harsh speech. This is specious talk, this is the retribution for spe-

117

cious talk. This is greed, this is the retribution for greed. This is wrath, this is the retribution for wrath.

" 'These are erroneous views, this is the retribution for erroneous views. This is stinginess, this is the retribution for stinginess. This is breaking the precepts, this is the retribution for breaking the precepts. This is anger, this is the retribution for anger. This is sloth, this is the retribution for sloth. This is distractedness, this is the retribution for distractedness. This is stupidity, this is the retribution for stupidity.

" 'This is accepting the precepts, this is keeping the precepts, this is violating the precepts. This is what ought to be done, this is what ought not to be done. This is creating obstacles, this is not creating obstacles. This is incurring blame, this is avoiding blame. This is purity, this is defilement. This is to have outflows, this is to be free of outflows. This is the wrong way, this is the correct way. This is the conditioned, this is the unconditioned. This is the mundane world, this is nirvana.'

"These people who are difficult to convert have minds like monkeys. Therefore one must resort to various methods in order to control and regulate their minds. Only then can they be tamed and made obedient. It is like dealing with an elephant or horse that is wild and unruly. One must apply sharp blows, till it feels them in its bones, and then it can be tamed. And it is the same with these stubborn and strong-willed beings who are difficult to convert. Therefore one uses all sorts of bitter and piercing words, and then they can be made to observe the precepts."

When those bodhisattvas had finished listening to this explanation, they all exclaimed, "We have never heard of such a thing before! A World-Honored One like Shakyamuni who conceals his immeasurable powers of freedom and preaches the Law in a manner that will please the mean in spirit in order to save and liberate all beings! And these bodhisattvas—how zealous of them, in their immeasurably great pity, to condescend to be born in this Buddha land!"

118

Vimalakirti said, "The bodhisattvas of this land are indeed steadfast in their great pity for all living beings. It is just as you have said. And the enrichment and benefit they bring to living beings in one lifetime here is greater than that bestowed in other worlds over the space of a hundred thousand kalpas. Why? Because in this saha world there are ten good practices that do not exist in any of those pure lands.

"What are these ten? Almsgiving, which does away with poverty and destitution. Pure precepts, which do away with violation of the prohibitions. Forbearance, which does away with anger. Assiduousness, which does away with sloth. Meditation, which does away with distractedness of mind. Wisdom, which does away with stupidity. The explanation of how to remove oneself from difficulties, which saves those who face the eight difficulties. The doctrine of the Great Vehicle, which saves those who delight in the Lesser Vehicle. The cultivation of good roots, which rescues those who are lacking in virtue. And the four ways of winning people, which are constantly employed to guide living beings to success. These are the ten."

The bodhisattvas said, "What methods must these bodhisattvas carry out in their practices in this saha world so that they may be born free of boils and sores in a pure land?"[2]

Vimalakirti replied, "These bodhisattvas must carry out eight methods in their practices in this world in order to be born free of boils and sores in a pure land. What are these eight? They must enrich and benefit living beings but look for no recompense. They must take upon themselves the sufferings of all living beings, and what merit they acquire thereby shall all be a gift to those beings. In mind they must be like other living beings, humbling themselves, descending to their level, erecting no barriers. They shall regard other bodhisattvas as though they

119

2. *That is, free of physical ills or defects. Such ills would indicate that the bodhisattva's religious practice had been faulty.*

were looking at the Buddha himself. When they hear a sutra they have not heard before, they shall not doubt it, and they shall not dispute with or oppose the voice-hearers. They shall not envy the alms received by others, nor boast of their own gains. In carrying out these methods, they must regulate and control their minds, constantly reflecting on their own faults and not censuring the shortcomings of others. At all times they shall with a single mind strive to acquire merits. These are the eight methods."

When Vimalakirti and Manjushri expounded these teachings to the great assembly, a hundred thousand heavenly and human beings all set their minds on attaining anuttara-samyak-sambodhi, and ten thousand bodhisattvas were able to accept the truth of birthlessness.

## Chapter 11

## ACTIONS OF THE BODHISATTVAS

At that time the Buddha was in the Amra Gardens preaching the Law when the ground suddenly became broad and beautifully adorned, and all the persons assembled there took on a golden color.

Ananda said to the Buddha, "World-Honored One, what is the reason for this auspicious sign? The area has become suddenly broadened and adorned, and the members of the assembly have all taken on a golden color!"

The Buddha said to Ananda, "Vimalakirti and Manjushri, reverently surrounded by a great gathering of persons, have decided to come here. Therefore this auspicious sign has first of all appeared."

At that moment Vimalakirti said to Manjushri, "Let us go together to see the Buddha and join the bodhisattvas in paying obeisance and making offerings."

Manjushri said, "Excellent, we will go indeed! This is just the time to do so."

Vimalakirti, employing his supernatural powers, proceeded to pick up the whole great assembly, along with their lion seats, place them in the palm of his right hand, and journey with them to the place where the Buddha was. After arriving there and depositing them on the ground, he bowed his head at the feet of the Buddha, circled to the right, performing seven circumambulations of the Buddha and, pressing his palms together with a single mind, stood to one side. The bodhisattvas all immediately left their seats, bowed their heads at the Buddha's feet, performed seven circumambulations, and stood to one side. The major disciples, Brahmas, Indras, and Four Heavenly Kings all likewise left their seats, bowed their heads at the Buddha's feet, and stood to one side.

Then the Buddha, after making the customary greetings and inquiries, sent them back to their seats. After all of them, following his instructions, had settled again in their seats, the Buddha said to Shariputra, "Did you see what these bodhisattvas, these great men, did through their freely exercised supernatural powers?"

"Yes, I saw it."

"And what did you think of it?"

"World-Honored One, what I saw them do was incredible. My mind cannot comprehend it, it is beyond my fathoming!"

At that time Ananda said to the Buddha, "World-Honored One, this fragrance I smell is like nothing I have ever known. What fragrance is this?"

The Buddha replied to Ananda, "This is the fragrance that comes from the pores of these bodhisattvas."

Then Shariputra said to Ananda, "Our pores too put forth this fragrance!"

"Where does it come from?" asked Ananda.

"It comes from the rice left over from the Buddha's meal that the rich man Vimalakirti had brought from the country Many Fragrances," replied Shariputra. "The pores of everyone who ate it at his house emit this kind of fragrance."

Then Ananda asked Vimalakirti, "How long will this fragrant aroma last?"

Vimalakirti said, "Until the rice is digested."

"And how long will it be before the rice is digested?"

"The power of this rice is such that it will be seven days before it is digested. Moreover, Ananda, if voice-hearers who have not yet reached the stage of ultimate determination eat this rice, they will be able to digest it only after they reach that stage. And if persons who have already reached that stage eat this rice, they will be able to digest it only after they have gained liberation of mind. If those who have not yet set their minds on attaining the Great Vehicle eat this rice, they will have to set their minds on that before they can digest it. If those who have already set their minds on doing so eat this rice, they will have to accept the truth of birthlessness before they can digest it. If those who have already accepted the truth of birthlessness eat this rice, they will have to advance to the place where Buddhahood is assured them in their next birth before they can digest it. It is like the medicine called Superior Flavor that remains undigested until all the poisons in the body of the person who takes it have been eliminated. This rice is the same—only after all the poisons of earthly desires have been wiped out will it be digested."

Ananda said to the Buddha, "I have never heard of such a thing, World-Honored One—to think that this fragrant rice can be used to do the Buddha's work!"

The Buddha said, "Just so, just so, Ananda. And there are some Buddha lands where the radiant light of the Buddha is used to do the Buddha's work. Some where bodhisattvas are used to do the Buddha's work. Some where phantom beings conjured up by the Buddha are used for the Buddha's work. Some where the bodhi tree is used for the Buddha's work. Some where the Buddha's garments or bedding are used for the Buddha's work. Some where the Buddha's food is used for the Buddha's work. Some where gardens, groves, pavilions, and towers are used to do the Buddha's work. Some where the thirty-two features and eighty characteristics, auspicious marks that accompany the body of the Buddha, are used to do the Buddha's work. Some where the Buddha's body is used for the Buddha's work. And some where empty space is used for the Buddha's work. Living beings, responding to these various agents, are thereby led to undertake the practice of the precepts.

"There are lands where similes such as dreams, phantoms, reflections, echoes, images in a mirror, the moon in the water, or

*123*

shimmering heat waves are used to do the Buddha's work. There are some where voices, spoken words, or written words are used to do the Buddha's work. Or pure Buddha lands where tranquil silence, without words, without explanations, without purport, without cognition, without action, without conditioning, does the Buddha's work. Thus, Ananda, among all daily activities of the Buddhas, their comings and goings, every act that they carry out, there is not one that does not do the Buddha's work.

"Ananda, there is a gate known as the four devils and the eighty-four thousand earthly desires. Living beings are wearied and belabored by these devils and desires, but the Buddhas use this as a method by which to do the Buddha's work. This is called the Dharma gate of entry to all Buddhas. Bodhisattvas who have entered this gate, when they see Buddha lands replete with all manner of purity and beauty, will not for that reason feel delight or longing or elation, and when they see Buddha lands with all sorts of impurities, they will not feel sad or vexed or downcast. They will merely regard the Buddhas with renewed purity of mind, experiencing a joy and reverence they have never known before. The merits of the various Buddhas, the Thus Come Ones, are all equal, but in order to convert living beings, they manifest themselves in different kinds of Buddha lands.

124 "Ananda, look at the various Buddha lands. The land in them is varied, but there is no variation in the sky. And it is the same when you look at the various Buddhas. Their physical bodies are varied, but that is all. There is no variation in their unimpeded wisdom. Ananda, a physical body, impressive features, lineage, precepts, meditation, wisdom, emancipations, the insight of emancipations, powers, fearlessnesses, properties not shared by others, great compassion, great pity, the observance of proper demeanor, as well as a fixed life span, the power to preach the Law, to teach and convert others, to lead living beings to enlightenment, to purify the Buddha lands, and to assimilate the Law

of other Buddhas—all these are possessed equally by all the various Buddhas. Therefore they are called Samyak-sambuddha (Perfectly Enlightened Buddha), they are called Tathagata (Thus Come One), they are called Buddha (Enlightened One).

"Ananda, if I were to explain to you in detail the meaning of these three epithets, you could live for a whole kalpa and still not hear all I have to say. Even if all the living beings in the thousand-millionfold world were like you, Ananda, who are foremost in hearing the teachings and concentrating on and retaining all you have heard, and they were to live for a whole kalpa, they could not hear it all. So it is, Ananda—the anuttara-samyak-sambodhi of the Buddhas is beyond fathoming, and their wisdom and eloquence defy comprehension."

Ananda said to the Buddha, "From now on, I will never dare think of myself as a person who has 'heard many of the teachings.' "

The Buddha said to Ananda, "Don't be discouraged! Why? Because when I spoke of you as foremost among the voice-hearers in the volume of teachings you have heard, I was not speaking with the bodhisattvas in mind. So do not take the matter to heart, Ananda. No wise person should try to estimate the abilities of the bodhisattvas. All the deepest places in the sea can still be fathomed, but the meditation, wisdom, power to retain the teachings, eloquence, and all the various merits of the bodhisattvas are immeasurable. Ananda, you and the others had best forget about the actions of the bodhisattvas. This manifestation of supernatural power that Vimalakirti has just now shown us no voice-hearer or pratyekabuddha could equal in a hundred thousand kalpas, no matter how he might exhaust his powers of transformation!"

Then the bodhisattvas who had come from the world Many Fragrances pressed their palms together and addressed the Buddha, saying, "World-Honored One, when we first saw this land, we thought of it as base and inferior. But now we regret our error and have put such thoughts out of our minds. Why? Because the expedient means employed by the Buddhas are beyond comprehension. In order to save living beings, they manifest different kinds of Buddha lands, depending upon what is appropriate to the circumstances. Very well then, World-Honored One. We would like you to bestow a little of your teachings on us so that when we return to our own land we will have something to remember the Thus Come One by."

The Buddha announced to the bodhisattvas, "There is the doctrine of the exhaustible and the inexhaustible emancipation. You would do well to learn this. What does exhaustible mean? It means those things that are conditioned. What does inexhaustible mean? It means those things that are unconditioned. But beings such as the bodhisattvas do not exhaust [or have done with] the conditioned, nor do they dwell in the unconditioned.

"What is meant by not exhausting the conditioned? It means not setting aside great compassion, not renouncing great pity; giving profound expression to the mind of comprehensive wisdom and never forgetting it; teaching and converting living beings without ever wearying; being constantly mindful of the four methods of winning people and applying them in season; guarding and upholding the correct Law without thought for life or limb. It means to work tirelessly to plant the roots of goodness; to keep the will at all times fixed on expedient means and the transfer of merit to others; to seek the Law without ever slacking, to preach the Law without ever stinting. It means diligently making offerings to the Buddhas; purposely entering the realm of birth and death with no feelings of fear; facing all types of honor or disgrace without thought of sadness or joy; not looking with contempt on those who have yet to learn and respecting the learned as though they were the Buddha himself. It means arousing correct thoughts in those sunk in earthly desires, but without unduly prizing the desire to remove oneself from passion. One should not cling to one's own desires, but applaud the desires of others.

"It means looking on meditational states as though they were a form of hell, but on the realm of birth and death as though contemplating a garden; viewing those who come seeking instruction with thoughts of how one may be a good teacher; setting aside one's own possessions and thinking how to acquire comprehensive wisdom; seeing those who violate the precepts and rousing thoughts of how to save them.

"It means thinking of the paramitas as one's father and mother; thinking of the elements of the Way as one's retinue of followers; working ceaselessly to nourish the roots of goodness; using the adornments of other pure lands to complete a Buddha land of one's own; practicing unbounded charity and thereby acquiring auspicious physical characteristics; putting aside all evil and purifying body, mouth, and mind; dwelling in the realm of birth and death for countless kalpas, ever valiant in mind; listening to the immeasurable virtues of the Buddha, one's determination never flagging; using the sword of wisdom to cut down the thieves of earthly desires; going beyond the realm of components, elements, and sense-media, shouldering the burden of living beings and bringing them to unending emancipation; employing great assiduousness in driving back and vanquishing the armies of the devil; constantly seeking to practice the wisdom that is without discriminative thought, the true aspect of reality; with regard to worldly things, lessening desires, knowing what is enough; with regard to unworldly things, tirelessly seeking them, and yet not rejecting the things of the world.

"It means never breaking the rules of proper demeanor, yet being able to accommodate to worldly ways; calling up transcendental powers and wisdom and using them to guide living beings; acquiring concentration and retention of memory so that one never forgets what one has heard; being able to distin-

127

guish the different capacities of people correctly and freeing them from doubt; expounding the Law with a pleasing and appropriate eloquence that flows unimpeded; scrupulously carrying out the ten good actions and receiving the blessings of human and heavenly beings; cultivating the four immeasurable qualities of mind and opening up the Brahma way; earnestly requesting to hear the preaching of the Law and receiving it with joy and commendation; acquiring the voice of the Buddha and the excellence of his body, mouth, and mind; acquiring his proper demeanor, practicing his good Law with profound diligence, ever more accomplished in action; using the Great Vehicle teachings to create a community of bodhisattvas; never self-indulgent in mind, never missing an opportunity for acts of goodness—one who practices these methods may be called a bodhisattva who does not exhaust the conditioned.

"What is meant by saying that the bodhisattva does not dwell in the unconditioned? It means that one studies and practices the teachings on emptiness, but does not take emptiness to be enlightenment. One studies and practices the teachings on nonform and nonaction, but does not take nonform and nonaction to be enlightenment. One studies and practices the teachings on nonarousal [of causes], but does not take nonarousal to be enlightenment. One views things as impermanent, but does not neglect to cultivate the roots of goodness. One views the world as marked by suffering, but does not hate to be born and die in it. One sees that there is no permanent ego, but is tireless in instructing others. One sees that there is such a thing as tranquil extinction, but does not dwell in extinction for long. One views the world as something to be cast off, withdrawn from, yet with body and mind one practices goodness. One sees there is no destination, yet one makes the good Law one's destination. One sees there is no birth, yet one takes on the form of birth in order to share the burdens of others. One sees that outflows [of passion] should be cut off, yet one does not cut them off. One sees that there is nothing to be practiced, yet one practices the Law in order to teach and convert living beings. One embraces the view of emptiness and nothingness, yet does not discard one's great pity. One embraces the view that the correct Law [nirvana] can be attained, yet one does not follow Lesser Vehicle doctrines in this matter. One embraces the view that all phenomena are void and false, lacking firmness, lacking personality, lacking a master, lacking form, yet while one's original vow remains unfulfilled, one does not regard merits, virtues, meditation, or wisdom as meaningless. When one practices these methods, one may be called a bodhisattva who does not dwell in the unconditioned."

At that time those bodhisattvas, having heard the explanation of this teaching, were all filled with great delight. Selecting from among the many wonderful flowers those of various colors and various fragrances, they scattered them throughout the whole thousand-millionfold world. And then, having made their offering to the Buddha and to these sutra teachings, as well as to the other bodhisattvas, they bowed their heads in obeisance at the Buddha's feet and sighed at having heard what they had never heard before, exclaiming, "Shakyamuni Buddha knows how to employ expedient means in a truly skillful manner!"

Having spoken these words, they suddenly vanished from sight and returned to their own country.

## Chapter 12

SEEING AKSHOBHYA BUDDHA

At that time the World-Honored One said to Vimalakirti, "You wanted to see the Thus Come One. Now how do you regard the Thus Come One?"

Vimalakirti said, "As I would regard my own true form or reality—in that same way do I regard the Thus Come One. I regard the Thus Come One as not existing from past times, not departing in the future, not abiding here at present.

"I do not regard him as form, I do not regard him as resembling form, I do not regard him as having the nature of form. I do not regard him as perception, conception, volition, or consciousness. I do not regard him as resembling consciousness. I do not regard him as having the nature of consciousness.[1]

"He does not rise out of the four great elements but is the same as the empty sky. He is without accumulation of the six sense-media, he has transcended eye, ear, nose, tongue, body, and mind, and does not exist in the threefold world. He has separated himself from the three defilements [of greed, anger, and stupidity], passed through the three gates to emancipation, and acquired the three understandings, which are the equivalent of ignorance.

"He is not identical in form with others, not different in form, not of his own form, not of some other form, not lacking form, not acquiring form. He is not on this shore, not on the other shore, not in midstream, and yet he converts living beings.

1. *Vimalakirti spells out the full process of negation only for the first and last of the five components, form and consciousness, but it is assumed that the same negations apply to the other three, perception, conception, and volition.*

He is seen to be in tranquil extinction, but does not remain in extinction for long. He is not this, he is not that, he does not show himself in this, he does not show himself in that. One cannot know him through wisdom, one cannot be conscious of him through consciousness. He is without darkness, without brightness, without name, without form, without strength, without weakness. He is not pure, not defiled, not in any direction, not removed from direction, not conditioned, not unconditioned, without purport, without explanation. He is not charitable, not stingy, does not observe the precepts, does not violate them, is not forbearing, not irate, does not press forward, does not slack, is not calm in mind, is not distracted, is not wise, is not stupid, is not sincere, is not deceitful, does not arrive, does not depart, does not go out, does not enter in. He is cut off from all that can be said in words.

"He is not a field that produces merit, not a field that does not produce merit, he is not worthy of alms, he is not unworthy of alms. He is not to be acquired, not to be put aside, does not possess form, is not without form. He is identical with the ultimate reality, one with the Dharma-nature.

"He cannot be labeled, cannot be measured, for he is beyond all labeling and measuring. He is not big, not little, not to be seen, not to be heard, not to be awakened to, not to be known. He is removed from all ties and bonds, equal to all wisdoms, identical with living beings, free of distinctions with regard to things. He is utterly without loss, without contamination, without anxiety, without action, without rousing, without birth, without extinction, without fear, without sorrow, without joy, without weariness, without attachment, without a past existence, without a future existence, without a present existence. No words or explanations whatsoever can distinguish and depict him.

"World-Honored One, the body of the Thus Come One is like this and this is the way I regard him. To regard in this manner is called correct regarding. To regard in any other is called erroneous regarding."

At that time Shariputra asked Vimalakirti, "Where did you die before you were reborn here?"

Vimalakirti said, "In the Law that you learned, is there any such thing as dying or being born?"

Shariputra replied, "No, there is no dying or being born."

"If all things are without the nature of dying or being born, then why do you ask where I died before I was reborn here? What is your opinion? Do phantom men and women conjured up by a magician know anything of dying or being born?"

"No, there is no dying or being born for them."

"And have you not heard the Buddha say that all things are in the nature of conjured beings?"

"Yes," replied Shariputra.

"If all things are in the nature of conjured beings, then why do you ask where I died before I was reborn here? Shariputra, dying is in its nature simply the destruction of something that is empty and fraudulent, and being born is in its nature the continuation of something that is empty and fraudulent. But the bodhisattva, though he dies, does not wipe out his good roots, and though he is born, he does not prolong those things that are evil."

At that time the Buddha said to Shariputra, "There is a country called Wonderful Joy with a Buddha named Immovable (Akshobhya). Vimalakirti here died in that country and was reborn in this one."

Shariputra said, "I have never heard of such a thing, World-Honored One! That this man could bring himself to abandon a land of purity and willingly come to this place with all its wrath and injury!"

Vimalakirti said to Shariputra, "What is your opinion? When the light of the sun shines forth, does it mix with the darkness?"

"No," replied Shariputra. "When the light of the sun shines forth, all darkness at once ceases to exist."

Vimalakirti said, "And the sun—why does it visit this continent of Jambudvipa?"

"Because it wishes to use its brightness to drive the darkness away," replied Shariputra.

Vimalakirti said, "The bodhisattva is like this. Though he is born in an impure Buddha land, he does this so he can convert living beings. He does not mix with or share its stupidity and darkness. He merely wipes out the darkness of earthly desires that besets living beings."

At that time the members of the great assembly were filled with longing, desiring to see the Wonderful Joy world and the Thus Come One Immovable and his host of bodhisattvas and voice-hearers. The Buddha knew what all the members of the assembly were thinking, and he said to Vimalakirti, "Good man, you must make the land Wonderful Joy and the Thus Come One Immovable and his host of bodhisattvas and voice-hearers visible to the members of this assembly. They all long to see them!"

Then Vimalakirti thought to himself, "Now, without rising from my seat, I shall take this country Wonderful Joy, with its Iron Encircling Mountains and rivers, its valleys, waterways, great seas, fountains, its Sumeru and the other mountains, along with its sun, moon, stars, the palaces of the heavenly beings, dragons, spirits, Brahmas and Indras, as well as its host of bodhisattvas and voice-hearers, its cities, villages, men and women, old and young, along with the Thus Come One Immovable and the bodhi trees and wonderful lotus blossoms that are able to carry out the Buddha's work in the ten directions, the jeweled straircases that extend from the continent of Jambudvipa all the way up to the Trayastrimsha heaven, the jeweled stairways by which the heavenly beings may descend and all pay reverence to the Thus Come One Immovable and listen to and receive his sutra teachings, and the inhabitants of Jambudvipa may also ascend these stairways to the Trayastrimsha heaven and visit its heavenly beings, for the world Wonderful Joy is replete with

133

immeasurable merits such as these, extending upward to the Akanishtha heaven and downward to its watery base—and all this I shall lift from its place and take in my right hand, as though removing it from a potter's wheel, and bring it here to this world, like some flower garland I am holding, and show it to all these beings!"

Having had this thought, he entered samadhi and, manifesting his transcendental powers, lifted the Wonderful Joy world out of its place with his right hand and set it down on the ground [in this world].

The host of bodhisattvas and voice-hearers and the various heavenly and human beings in that world who had acquired transcendental knowledge all cried out together, saying, "Look, World-Honored One! Someone is making off with us! Save and protect us, we beg of you!" But the Buddha Immovable said, "This is not my doing. This is the work of Vimalakirti's supernatural powers." And the rest of the beings in that world who had not yet acquired transcendental knowledge did not even realize or know where they had gotten to. But although the Wonderful Joy world had been placed on the ground in this world, it had not increased or decreased in size, and this world likewise had in no way become cramped or narrow, but was no different from what it had always been.

134    Then Shakyamuni Buddha addressed his great assembly, saying, "Do you see the Wonderful Joy world, the Thus Come One Immovable, and the splendid adornments of his land, the purity of the practices carried out by his bodhisattvas, the impeccable cleanness of his major disciples?"

All replied, "Yes, we have seen them."

The Buddha said, "If bodhisattvas wish to acquire a Buddha land as pure and spotless as this, they should study the way practiced by the Thus Come One Immovable."

When this Wonderful Joy country appeared in the saha world, fourteen nayutas of persons set their minds on attaining anuttara-samyak-sambodhi, all desiring to be born in the Buddha land Wonderful Joy. Shakyamuni thereupon gave them a prophecy, saying, "You will be born in that land."

Then the Wonderful Joy world, having finished bestowing enrichment and benefit upon this country, returned to its original place. All the members of the assembly saw it do so.

The Buddha addressed Shariputra, saying, "Did you see this Wonderful Joy world and the Buddha Immovable?"

"Yes, I saw them, World-Honored One. And I beg you to enable all living beings to acquire a clean and pure land like that of the Buddha Immovable, and to gain transcendental powers like those of Vimalakirti.

"World-Honored One, I and the others have happily acquired excellent benefits, being able to see this person and to approach and make offerings to him. And other living beings, either now while the Buddha is here or after he has passed away, if they hear this sutra, will acquire excellent benefits as well. And how much more so if, having heard it, they believe and understand it, accept and uphold it, read and recite it, expound it to others, and practice it as the Law directs. One who holds this sutra in hand has thereby acquired the storehouse of the jewels of the Law. If one reads and recites it, understands and expounds it, and practices it as the Law directs, the Buddhas will guard and keep in mind that person. And if there are those who give alms to such a person, let it be known that this is giving alms to the Buddha. If there are those who copy and preserve these sutra scrolls, let it be known that the Thus Come One will visit their rooms. And if there are those who, hearing this sutra, can respond with appropriate joy, those persons will forthwith acquire comprehensive wisdom. If there are those who believe and understand this sutra, even just one four-line verse of it, and can expound it to others, let it be known that such persons will forthwith receive a prophecy of the attainment of anuttara-samyak-sambodhi."

## Chapter 13

## THE OFFERING OF THE LAW

At that time Shakra Devanam (Indra) spoke up from the great assembly, addressing the Buddha in these words, "World-Honored One, though I have heard hundreds and thousands of sutras from the Buddha and Manjushri, I have never heard one with such astounding freedom of action, transcendental powers, and unfailing grasp of the true reality. According to my understanding of what the Buddha has just said, if there are living beings who hear this sutra on the Law, believe and understand it, accept and uphold it, read and recite it, then they will surely and without doubt acquire that Law. And how much more so if they practice it as the Law directs. Such persons will shut off all evil paths of existence and open the gates to all good ones. They will be constantly guarded and kept in mind by the Buddhas, will refute the non-Buddhist teachings, overcome the devil and his animosity, cultivate and practice bodhi, and rest secure in the place of practice, following in the way trod by the Thus Come One.

"World-Honored One, if there are persons who accept and uphold, read and recite this sutra and practice it as the Law directs, then I and my followers will offer alms to them and serve them. And if there is a place among the villages or towns, the mountain forests or the broad plain where this sutra exists, then I and my followers will go there together to listen to and accept the Law; and those who do not yet believe in it I will lead to belief, and to those who already believe I will be a guardian."

The Buddha said, "Excellent, excellent, heavenly lord! It is just as you have said. And I will assist you in your joyful task. This sutra expounds in comprehensive manner the anuttara-samyak-sambodhi of the Buddhas of the past, future, and present, which is beyond comprehension. Therefore, heavenly lord, if good men and good women accept, uphold, read, recite, and make offerings to this sutra, they are making offering to the Buddhas of past, future, and present.

"Heavenly lord, suppose this thousand-millionfold world were as full of Thus Come Ones as it is of sugarcane, bamboo, reeds, rice and hemp plants, or forest trees. If there were good men or good women who for the space of a kalpa, or less than a kalpa, were to revere and honor, praise and make offerings to them and provide for their well-being; and if after those Buddhas had passed away, these persons built towers adorned with the seven treasures to house the relics from each Buddha body, towers so broad they covered the four continents and so high they reached to the Brahma heaven, their central pole richly decorated; and if these persons made offerings of all kinds of flowers, incense, necklaces, flags, pennants, and music, all of the most refined and wonderful kind, and did this for the space of a kalpa, or less than a kalpa—heavenly lord, what is your opinion? Would these persons have thereby planted the seeds of many blessings?"

Shakra Devanam replied, "Of many blessings indeed, World-Honored One! If I were to spend a hundred thousand million kalpas, I could never finish describing all their blessings and merits."

The Buddha said to the heavenly lord, "You should under-  137
stand that if there are good men and good women who, on hearing this sutra on the emancipation Beyond Comprehension, believe, understand, accept, uphold, read, recite, and practice it, their blessings will be even greater than those of such persons. Why? Because the bodhi of the Buddhas is all born from this sutra. The marks of bodhi are beyond limit or measure, and for that reason their blessings are immeasurable."

The Buddha then said to the heavenly lord, "A countless asamkhya number of kalpas in the past, there appeared in the world a Buddha named Medicine King, Thus Come One, worthy of offerings, of right and universal knowledge, perfect clarity and conduct, well gone, understanding the world, unexcelled worthy, trainer of people, teacher of heavenly and human beings, Buddha, World-Honored One.[1] His world was called Great Adornment and his kalpa was called Adornment. This Buddha had a life span of twenty small kalpas. His voice-hearer monks numbered thirty-six million nayutas and his bodhisattva monks twelve million.

"Heavenly lord, at that time there was a wheel-turning sage king named Jeweled Parasol who possessed all the seven treasures and ruled over the four continents of the world. This king had a thousand sons, upright, valiant, capable of overpowering their enemies. At that time Jeweled Parasol came with his followers to make offerings to the Thus Come One Medicine King, providing him with all he needed for his well-being. He did this for five whole kalpas, and when the five kalpas were over, he said to his sons, 'You too should make offerings to the Buddha with the same deeply searching mind as I have shown.' The thousand sons, obeying their father's command, proceeded to make offerings to the Thus Come One Medicine King for another five full kalpas, providing him with everything needed for his well-being.

"One of the king's sons named Moon Parasol sat all alone, thinking to himself, 'Isn't there some offering that is better than these?'

"Then, through the Buddha's supernatural power, a heavenly being appeared in the sky and said, 'Good man, the offering of the Law is the finest of all offerings!'

"The son asked, 'What is the offering of the Law?'

"The heavenly being replied, 'You should go and ask the Thus Come One Medicine King. He will explain to you in detail the offering of the Law.'

---

1. *The phrases following the name of the Buddha constitute the conventional ten epithets or honorable titles for a Buddha.*

"At once the prince Moon Parasol went to call on the Thus Come One Medicine King. After bowing his head in obeisance at the Buddha's feet, he retired to one side and addressed the Buddha, saying, 'World-Honored One, among all offerings, the offering of the Law is the finest. But what is the offering of the Law?'

"The Buddha said, 'Good man, the offering of the Law means the profound sutras preached by the Buddhas. The people of this world all find them hard to believe and hard to accept, for they are wonderfully subtle and hard to make out, clean and pure and without stain. They cannot be grasped through the making of distinctions or through thought. They are contained in the storehouse of the bodhisattva and are sealed with the dharani seal,[2] and where this seal is affixed, one reaches the level of no regression. They bring about observance of the six paramitas, the skillful discrimination of meanings, and compliance with the teachings of bodhi, and through the finest of all sutras one enters the realm of great pity and compassion. The sutras put an end to all devilish affairs and all erroneous views, conform to the teaching on causality and those on no ego, no individual, no living beings, no life span, emptiness, no form, no action, and no arousing. They enable living beings to sit in the place of practice and to turn the wheel of the Law.

" 'Heavenly beings, dragons, spirits, gandharvas, and the others join in praising them. They can enable living beings to enter the storehouse of the Buddha Law; they embrace the comprehensive wisdom of the worthies and sages and expound the way practiced by the bodhisattvas. Relying on the principle of the true nature of all phenomena, they clearly set forth the doctrines of impermanence, suffering, emptiness, no ego, and tranquil extinction. They can save all living beings who violate the prohibitions, and in all devils, non-Buddhist believers, and those

---

2. *The seal of memory that insures full retention of the teachings.*

given to greed and attachment they can inspire fear. Buddhas, worthies, and sages join in extolling them. They turn away from the sufferings of birth and death and show instead the joy of nirvana. They are preached by the Buddhas of the ten directions and the three existences of past, present, and future.

" 'If one hears sutras such as these, believes, understands, accepts, upholds, reads, and recites them, and by employing the power of expedient means makes distinctions and expounds them for the sake of living beings, rendering their meaning perfectly clear, one is thereby guarding and protecting the Law, and this is called the offering of the Law.

" 'Again, the sutras enable one to practice the teachings as the Law directs, to accord with the twelve-linked chain of causation, to set aside erroneous views and accept the truth of birthlessness, to realize once and for all that there is no ego, no existence of living beings, no deviating from or disputing with the law of cause and effect, thus removing all thought of personal possession.

" 'They teach one to rely on meaning, not on words; to rely on wisdom, not on consciousness; to rely on sutras that are complete in meaning, not on those that are incomplete in meaning; to rely on the Law, not on the person; to go along with the true form of things, realizing that there is no entering in and no destination. They teach that, since ignorance in the end does not exist, so too action in the end does not exist, and so on through the other links in the twelve-linked chain of causation down to the fact that, since birth in the end does not exist, so too old age and death in the end do not exist. And when one learns to see in this manner, the twelve-linked chain of causation will cease to have any form that comes to an end, and one will no longer entertain the view that it does. This is called the finest of all offerings of the Law.' "

The Buddha [Shakyamuni] then said to the heavenly lord, "When Prince Moon Parasol heard Medicine King Buddha expound the Law in this manner, he acquired a compliant tolerance of the truth of birthlessness. At once he took off his jeweled robes and the ornaments that adorned his body and offered them to the Buddha, saying, 'World-Honored One, after the Thus Come One has passed into extinction, I will carry out offerings of the Law and guard the correct Law. I beg you, through your might and supernatural powers, to take pity on me and strengthen me so that I can conquer the devil and his enmity and practice the bodhisattva way.'

"The Buddha knew the thoughts that were in his deeply searching mind and bestowed on him a prophecy, saying, 'In that latter age you will guard and protect the citadel of the Law.'

"Heavenly lord, at that time Prince Moon Parasol, observing the purity of the Law and hearing this prophecy bestowed by the Buddha, was moved by faith to leave the household life and take up the practice of the good Law. He had not devoted himself to diligent practice for long when he was able to acquire the five transcendental powers, carry out the bodhisattva way, and gain dharani power and unflagging eloquence. After the Buddha had passed into extinction, he exercised the transcendental powers he had acquired, the power to retain all he had heard, and the eloquence for fully ten small kalpas, continuing to turn the wheel of the Law turned by the Thus Come One Medicine King and spreading the teachings abroad. This monk Moon Parasol, by guarding and protecting the Law and putting forth diligent effort, was able in the space of his lifetime to convert hundreds, thousands, millions of persons, insuring that they would never regress in their pursuit of anuttara-samyak-sambodhi; to cause fourteen nayutas of others to develop a profound aspiration for the way of the voice-hearer or the pratyekabuddha; and to enable countless living beings to be born in the heavenly realm.

141

"Heavenly lord, the person who was king Jeweled Parasol at the time I have been speaking of—what do you think? He has now become a Buddha named Jewel Flame Thus Come One. And the king's one thousand sons will become the thousand

Buddhas who will appear in our present age, the Worthy Kalpa.[3] Krakucchanda was the first to attain Buddhahood, and the last will be the Thus Come One named Ruchi. The monk Moon Parasol is none other than myself.

"Thus, heavenly lord, you should understand this important point. The offering of the Law is the finest of all offerings. It is first in rank and without equal. Therefore, heavenly lord, you should use this offering of the Law as your offering to the Buddha."

---

3. *Various sutras predict that a thousand Buddhas will appear in our present kalpa or eon, which is accordingly termed the Worthy Kalpa. Shakyamuni is the fourth to appear, and Maitreya will be the fifth.*

*Chapter 14*

Then the Buddha addressed the bodhisattva Maitreya, saying, "Maitreya, I now take this Law of anuttara-samyak-sambodhi, gathered over countless millions of asamkhya kalpas, and entrust it to you. In the latter age after the Buddha has passed into extinction, you must employ your supernatural powers to propagate sutras such as this, spreading them throughout the continent of Jambudvipa and never allowing them to be wiped out. Why? Because in the ages to come there will be good men and good women, as well as heavenly beings, dragons, spirits, gandharvas, rakshasas, and others, who will set their minds on attaining anuttara-samyak-sambodhi and will delight in the great Law. If they are unable to hear sutras such as this, they will lose the opportunity to gain excellent benefits. But if beings such as these hear these sutras, they will surely believe and delight greatly in them and set their minds on a rare achievement. Therefore you must respectfully accept these and, considering how living beings can best gain benefits from them, expound them far and wide.

"Maitreya, you should understand that there are two types of bodhisattvas. What are these two types? The first type loves varied phrases and literary embellishment. The second is not afraid of deeper principles and is able to enter into the true meaning. If there are those who love varied phrases and literary embellishments, you may be sure that they are beginners in the bodhisattva way. But if there are those who, approaching these extremely profound sutras, with their teachings on nondefilement and nonattachment, are not timid or fearful but can enter into the meaning and, having heard the sutras, with pure minds

143

will accept, uphold, read, and recite them and practice them as the Law directs, you may be sure that they have been practicing the way for a long time.

"Again, Maitreya, there are two attitudes among those called beginners that prevent them from getting a firm grasp on these extremely profound teachings. What are these two? First is that of persons who, when they hear some profound sutra they have not heard before, are alarmed and timorous and, giving way to doubt, cannot bring themselves to comply with it. In their disbelief they speak slanderously of it, saying, 'I have never heard this before! Where does it come from?' Second is that of persons who, though there are those who guard, uphold, understand, and expound profound sutras of this type, are unwilling to associate closely with them, to offer them alms or treat them with respect, but at times may even speak of their faults before others. Where you find these two attitudes, you may be sure the persons are beginners in the bodhisattva way. They do injury to themselves and cannot train their minds to accept the profound teachings.

"Again, Maitreya, there are two attitudes among the bodhisattvas who, though they believe and understand the profound teachings, yet do injury to themselves and are unable to accept the truth of birthlessness. What are these two? First is that of persons who are contemptuous of beginner bodhisattvas and will not teach or enlighten them. Second is that of persons who, though they understand the profound teachings, seize upon surface appearances and make distinctions. These are the two attitudes."

The bodhisattva Maitreya, after listening to these words of exposition, addressed the Buddha, saying, "World-Honored One, this is something I have never heard before. It is as the Buddha has said. I must remove myself far off from evils such as these and strive to uphold this Law of anuttara-samyak-sambodhi that the Thus Come One has gathered over numberless asamkhya kalpas. If in the ages to come there are good men and good women who seek the Great Vehicle, I will see to it that sutras such as this come into their hands, will lend them powers of memorization, and will cause them to accept, uphold, read, and recite the sutras and expound them far and wide for others. World-Honored One, if in that latter age there are those who can accept, uphold, read, and recite them and expound them for others, you should know that all of them do so because I have inspired and strengthened them with my supernatural powers."

The Buddha said, "Excellent, excellent, Maitreya! It is as you have said. And the Buddha will assist you in your joyful task,"

With this all the bodhisattvas, pressing their palms together, said to the Buddha, "After the Thus Come One has passed into extinction, we too will spread the Law of anuttara-samyak-sam-bodhi far and wide throughout the lands in the ten directions and will guide and assist those who expound the Law, seeing to it that they acquire this sutra."

Then the Four Heavenly Kings said to the Buddha, "World-Honored One, in the towns and villages, the mountain forests and the broad plain, wherever there are those who possess this sutra, read and recite it, understand and expound it, we will take our ranks of officials and underlings and go to where they are so that we may hear the Law and will shelter and protect them, making certain that no one approaches within a hundred yojanas of them on any side to try to take unfair advantage of them"

Then the Buddha said to Ananda, "You must accept and uphold this sutra and propagate it far and wide."

Ananda replied, "Indeed I will! I have already accepted and upheld its essentials, World-Honored One. But by what name should this sutra be called?"

The Buddha said, "Ananda, this sutra should be called The Expositions of Vimalakirti. And another name for it is The Doctrine of the Emancipation Beyond Comprehension. This is how you should accept and uphold it."

When the Buddha had finished expounding this sutra, the rich man Vimalakirti, Manjushri, Shariputra, Ananda, and the others, along with the heavenly and human beings, asuras, and all the other members of the great assembly were filled with joy at hearing the preaching of the Buddha, [and they believed and accepted it and respectfully put it into practice.][1]

1. *The concluding passage in brackets is lacking in some versions of the text.*

The glossary contains definitions of all important personal and place names in the translation, as well as major Sanskrit terms and numerical categories. Sanskrit words are given with full diacritical marks when that form differs from the one in which the word appears in the translation. Skt = Sanskrit; Ch = Chinese; J = Japanese.

*Akanishtha (Akaniṣṭha) heaven.* The highest heaven in the world of form. Beings in this heaven possess a pure body, free from all suffering and illness.

*Akshobhya (Akṣobhya).* A Buddha mentioned in chapters 7 and 12. His name, which means "immovable," is rendered in Chinese as Wu-tung. He dwells in the eastern region and is especially important in Esoteric Buddhism.

*Amita.* The Sanskrit Amita, "infinite," stands for Amitābha, "infinite light," or Amitāyus, "infinite life." The name of a Buddha mentioned in chapter 7. He resides in a pure land in the west and is the central figure in the Pure Land teachings of Chinese and Japanese Buddhism.

*Amra (Āmra) Gardens.* Also known as the Āmrapālī or Āmbapālī Gardens. Gardens on the outskirts of Vaishali, presented to the Buddha and his followers by a courtesan of the city named Āmrapālī. The word āmra means mango.

*Ananda (Ānanda).* Cousin of Shakyamuni and one of his ten major disciples. He accompanied Shakyamuni for many years as his personal attendant and heard more of his teachings than any other disciple. He is accordingly known as foremost in hearing the Buddha's teachings. At the First Council held after Shakyamuni's death to put in order his teachings, Ananda is said to have recited the sutras from memory. The words "This is what I heard" that appear at the beginning of most sutras refer to this recitation.

147

*Aniruddha.* Cousin of Shakyamuni and one of his ten major disciples, known as foremost in divine insight.

*anuttara-samyak-sambodhi (anuttara-samyak-saṃbodhi).* Supreme perfect enlightenment, the enlightenment of a Buddha.

*arhat.* A "worthy," one who has attained the highest stage of Hinayana enlightenment, the highest of four kinds of voice-hearers. Such a person has gained freedom from transmigration in the six paths of existence. Mahayana Buddhism urges one to reject the goal of arhat and instead strive for the highest level of enlightenment, that of Buddhahood.

*asamkhya (asaṃkhya).* An ancient Indian numerical unit indicating an uncountably large number.

*asura.* A class of contentious demons in India mythology who fight continually with the god Indra. In Buddhism the asuras constitute one of the eight kinds of nonhuman beings who protect Buddhism.

*auspicious marks.* Remarkable physical characteristics possessed by Buddhas and other beings of great spiritual excellence. See also thirty-two features.

*bodhi.* Enlightenment or Buddhahood.

*bodhi tree.* The pipal tree of Buddhagayā under which Shakyamuni attained enlightenment.

*bodhisattva.* A being who aspires to attain Buddhahood and carries out various altruistic practices in order to achieve that goal. Compassion is the outstanding characteristic of the bodhisattva, who postpones his or her own entry into nirvana in order to assist others to gain enlightenment. The bodhisattva figure is particularly important in Mahayana Buddhism.

*Brahma king.* A king of the Brahma heaven, a deity who has attained supremacy in a particular universe. In Mahayana sutras such as the Vimalakirti the Brahma kings are vast in number.

*Brahma path.* Another name for the four immeasurable qualities, *q.v.*

*chain of causation.* See twelve-linked chain of causation.

*dharani (dhāranī).* A spell or formula said to protect one who recites it and benefit the person by virtue of its mystic power. The word literally means "to preserve and uphold" the Buddha's teachings in one's mind, hence it is associated with the power of memory.

*Dharma/dharma (Ch fa, J hō).* The Sanskrit word *dharma* has a wide range of meanings. When it appears in the translation or in the explanatory material here, it has one of three meanings: (1) The Buddhist doctrine or teachings; often translated as the Law. (2) The reality or truth revealed in the Buddhist teachings, the absolute. When used in either of these two meanings, the word has been capitalized and appears as Dharma. (3) The countless things or phenomena that make up existence. When used in this meaning it is written with a small "d": dharma.

*Dharma body.* See three bodies.

*Dharma-nature.* The underlying nature of all things, the absolute.

*eight difficulties.* Eight conditions under which it is difficult to see a Buddha or hear the Law. They are: (1) when one is in hell, (2) when one is a beast, (3) when one is a hungry spirit, (4) when one is in a heaven of long life, (5) when one is in the continent north of Mt. Sumeru, (6) when one is deaf, blind, and mute, (7) when one is complacent in worldly wisdom, and (8) when one lives in a time or place where there is no Buddha.

*eight emancipations.* They are: emancipation from the view that the body is pure, from the view that the outside world is pure, from illusions, from the view that matter exists, from the view that consciousness has limits, from the view that a thing has its own property, from the view that thought exists or that thought does not exist, and from the view that mentality exists in any sense.

*eight errors.* The opposite of the eight items of the eightfold path, *q.v.*

*eighteen sense-realms.* The six sense-media (definition 1), plus their six objects and the element of consciousness added to each of the six objects.

*eighteen unshared properties.* Properties possessed by a Buddha and not shared by others. They are: freedom from illusions, eloquence, absence of attachments, impartiality, constant concentration of mind, knowledge of all things, untiring intention to lead beings to salvation, incessant endeavor, consistency of teachings with those of other Buddhas, perfect wisdom, perfect emancipation, perfect insight, consistency of deeds with wisdom, consistency of words with wisdom, consistency of mind with wisdom, knowledge of the past, knowledge of the future, and knowledge of the present.

*eightfold holy path.* Right views, right thinking, right speech, right action, right way of life, right endeavor, right mindfulness, and right meditation. Part of the thirty-seven elements of the Way.

*eighty characteristics.* Extraordinary features that only Buddhas and bodhisattvas possess. There are various explanations of the eighty characteristics; some of the characteristics duplicate the thirty-two features.

*expedient means. (Skt upāya, Ch fang-pien, J hōben)* Skillful expedient methods devised by Buddhas and bodhisattvas to relieve others from suffering and lead them to enlightenment.

*five cardinal sins.* Killing one's father, killing one's mother, killing an arhat, causing injury to a Buddha, and disrupting the harmony of the order.

*five components.* Also called five skandas or five aggregates; components that in association make up most living beings. Form, perception, conception, volition, and consciousness.

*five desires.* The desires that arise from the contact of the five sense organs—eyes, ears, nose, tongue, and body—with their respective objects. Sometimes the five desires are defined as the desires for wealth, sex, food and drink, fame, and sleep.

*five eyes.* Five different faculties of vision: (1) the physical eye, (2) the divine eye, (3) the wisdom eye, (4) the Dharma eye, and (5) the Buddha eye.

*five impurities.* Sometimes called the five defilements; they are: (1) the impurity of the age, such as war or other disruptions of the social or natural environment; (2) impurity of desire, the tendency to be ruled by emotions such as greed and anger; (3) impurity of living beings, the physical and spiritual decline of human beings; (4) impurity of view, deriving from mistaken views or values; and (5) impurity of life span, the distortion of life itself, which leads to a disordered and shortened life span.

*five obscurations.* Five mental impediments that hinder meditation: greed, anger, depression and languor, agitation and regret, and doubt.

*five powers.* Five powers gained through the five roots of goodness. Part of the thirty-seven elements of the Way.

*five realms of existence.* The five lower paths or realms of existence, those of hell dwellers, hungry spirits, beasts, asuras, and human beings.

*five roots of goodness.* Faith, effort, mindfulness, concentration, and wisdom. Part of the thirty-seven elements of the Way.

*four bases of supernatural power.* Intense concentration of will, intense concentration of mind, intense concentration of effort, intense concentration of analysis. Part of the thirty-seven elements of the Way.

*Four Heavenly Kings.* Known in Sanskrit as lokapalās or World-Protectors, they serve Indra as his generals and guard the four continents that surround Mt. Sumeru. In Buddhism they serve as protectors of the Dharma.

*four immeasurable qualities.* Immeasurable pity, immeasurable compassion, immeasurable joy in helping all beings to become free of suffering, and immeasurable indifference in rising above all emotions and distinctions. Possession of these qualities insures one of birth in the Brahma heaven.

*four kinds of devils.* The demons of earthly desires, of the five components, of death, and of the heavenly realm.

*four kinds of fearlessness.* Four aspects of the Buddha's fearlessness in preaching. The Buddha is fearless in declaring that he is enlightened to the truth of all phenomena; fearless in proclaiming he has extinguished all desires and illusions; fearless in teaching that desires and karma can be obstacles to enlightenment; and fearless in teaching that one can overcome all sufferings by practicing Buddhism.

*four meditations.* Four stages of meditation that enable one to be favored by bliss in the world of form.

*four methods of winning people.* Four methods employed by bodhisattvas to attract others to their teachings. They are to give alms and expound the Law; to speak in a kindly manner; to work to benefit others; and to share their hardships and cooperate with them.

*four noble truths.* A fundamental doctrine of early Buddhism, it teaches that (1) all existence is marked by suffering; (2) suffering is caused by craving; (3) by doing away with craving one can gain release from suffering; (4) there is a method for achieving this goal. The method is that known as the eightfold path, which enjoins one to cultivate right views, right thinking, right speech, right action, right way of life, right endeavor, right mindfulness, and right meditation.

*four stages of mindfulness.* A Hinayana procedure for quieting the mind by contemplating the body as impure, sensation as always leading to suffering, the mind as impermanent, and things as being dependent in nature. Part of the thirty-seven elements of the Way.

*four topsy-turvy views.* Mistaking the impermanent for the permanent, the selfless for the self-possessing, the impure for the pure, and the miserable for the happy.

*four types of correct effort.* Efforts to put an end to existing sin or evil, to prevent evil from arising, to bring good into existence, and to encourage existing good. Part of the thirty-seven elements of the Way.

*gandharva.* A heavenly musician, one of the eight kinds of nonhuman beings who protect Buddhism.

*garuda (garuḍa).* In Indian mythology, a giant bird that is said to feed on dragons. One of the eight kinds of nonhuman beings who protect Buddhism.

*Great Vehicle.* See Mahayana.

*Hinayana (Hinayāna, Ch hsiao-ch'eng, J shōjō).* The term *Hinayana* or "Lesser Vehicle" is used by followers of the Mahayana teachings to designate the other major branch of Buddhism. Hinayana teaches that, since Buddhahood is almost impossible to attain, one should aim for a "lesser" goal, that of arhat. It is the form of Buddhism that prevails today in Sri Lanka, Burma, Thailand, Cambodia, and Laos, where it is known as Theravāda or the Teaching of the Elders.

*Indra.* Originally the god of thunder in Indian mythology, he was later incorporated into Buddhism as a disciple of the Buddha and protector of the Dharma and its followers. Also called Shakra (Śakra). As in the case of Brahma, the Indras are depicted as vast in number.

*Jambudvipa (Jambudvīpa).* The continent lying to the south of Mt. Sumeru, the "continent of the jambu trees," one of the four continents that make up a world. It is populated by people with bad karma; hence, Buddhism spreads there in order to bring them to salvation.

*kalpa.* An extremely long period of time.

*kimnara (kiṃnara).* A type of being who excels in singing and dancing and has a horse's head and a man's body. One of the eight kinds of nonhuman beings who protect Buddhism.

*Krakucchanda.* First of the thousand Buddhas that the sutras predict will appear in our present kalpa, the Worthy Kalpa.

*kshatriya (kṣatriya).* The warrior or ruler class in ancient India.

*Kumarajiva (Kumārajīva, 344–413 C.E.).* Central Asian scholar-monk who, with the aid of Chinese assistants, translated many Buddhist works into Chinese.

*Lesser Vehicle.* See Hinayana.

*Mahakashyapa (Mahākāśyapa).* One of Skakyamuni's ten major disciples, known as foremost in ascetic practice. After Shakyamuni's death, he became head of the order.

*Mahakatyayana (Mahākātyāyana).* One of Shakyamuni's ten major disciples, known as foremost in debate.

*Mahayana (Mahāyāna, Ch ta-ch'eng, J daijō).* One of the two main branches of Buddhism. It calls itself Mahayana or the "Great Vehicle" because its teachings enable all beings to attain Buddhahood. It lays particular emphasis upon the bodhisattva, who vows to attain Buddhahood for himself and to assist all others to do so. The Mahayana teachings arose around the first century B.C.E. and first century C.E. in India and spread to China, Tibet, Korea, Japan, and Vietnam.

*mahoraga.* A being with the head of a snake, one of the eight kinds of nonhuman beings who protect Buddhism.

*Maitreya.* A bodhisattva who figures prominently in the Vimalakirti Sutra. It is said that he will succeed Shakyamuni as the Buddha of the future and that he will appear in this world 5,670 million years after Shakyamuni's death. Meanwhile, according to tradition, he dwells in the Tushita heaven.

*Manjushri (Mañjuśrī).* A bodhisattva who figures prominently in the Vimalakirti Sutra. He is symbolic of the perfection of wisdom. In Buddhist art he is customarily depicted riding on a lion.

*Maudgalyayana (Maudgalyāyana).* One of Shakyamuni's ten major disciples, known as foremost in transcendental powers.

*Mount Sumeru.* See Sumeru.

*Narayana (Nārāyaṇa).* Another name for the god Vishnu in Indian mythology. Incorporated into Buddhism as a protective deity, he is represented in Buddhist scriptures as possessing great physical strength.

*nine sources of anxiety.* Nine mental distractions caused by thinking that someone has done injury to oneself, or to someone dear to oneself, or has served one's enemies, and imagining these three types of injuries as taking place in the three eras of past, present, and future.

*nirvana (nirvāṇa).* The word, which means "blown out," indicates the state in which one has escaped from the cycle of birth and death. In Mahayana Buddhism, it is taken to mean awakening to the true nature of phenomena, or the perfection of Buddha wisdom.

*Papiyas (Pāpīyas).* Another name for the Devil or Māra, a personification of evil.

*paramita.* See six paramitas.

*place of practice.* A place where one carries out religious practice and gains enlightenment, often referring specifically to the place where Shakyamuni gained enlightenment.

*pratyekabuddha.* A "self-enlightened" being, one who has won an understanding of the truth through his or her own efforts but makes no effort to enlighten others.

*Purna Maitrayaniputra (Pūrṇa Maitrāyaṇīputra).* Also known simply as Purna. One of Shakyamuni's ten major disciples, known as foremost in preaching the Law.

*Rahula (Rāhula).* The son of Shakyamuni and later one of his ten major disciples, known as foremost in inconspicuous practices.

*rakshasa (rākṣasa).* A type of evil demon who sometimes appears in Buddhist scriptures as a protector of Buddhism.

*Ruchi (Ruci).* Last of the thousand Buddhas that the sutras predict will appear in our present kalpa, the Worthy Kalpa.

*saha (sahā) world.* Our present world, which is full of suffering to be endured. The Sanskrit word *saha* means "endurance."

*samadhi (samādhi).* A state of intense concentration of mind, which produces a sense of inner serenity.

*samsara (saṃsāra).* The ordinary world of suffering and cyclical birth and death.

*sense-media.* See six sense-media.

*seven abodes of consciousness.* Seven categories of living beings, namely: beings who differ physically and intellectually; beings who differ physically but are similar intellectually; beings who are similar physically but differ intellectually; beings who are similar physically and intellectually; and three types of immaterial beings. These beings consist of humans, gods of the various realms of form, and beings in the realm of formlessness.

*seven assets.* Faith, observation of the precepts, almsgiving, wide knowledge, wisdom, an inward sense of shame, and a sense of shame before others.

*seven factors of enlightenment.* Discerning true from false, effort, joy, buoyancy, mindlessness, concentration, and indifference. Part of the thirty-seven elements of the Way.

*seven purities.* Purity in observance of the precepts, in mind, in views, in resolution of doubts, in discernment of paths, in knowledge and insight, and in nirvana.

*seven treasures.* Seven precious substances mentioned in Buddhist scriptures. The list varies from text to text, but is usually given as gold, silver, lapis lazuli, seashell, agate, pearl, and carnelian.

*Shakra or Shakra Devanam (Śakra Devānām).* Another name for Indra, *q.v.*

*Shariputra (Śāriputra).* One of Shakyamuni's ten major disciples, known as foremost in wisdom.

*Shikin (Śikhin).* Name of a Brahma king.

*six heretical teachers.* Six influential thinkers in India during Shakyamuni's time who openly broke with the old Vedic tradition and challenged Brahman authority in the Indian social order. They are referred to as "heretical" because their doctrines differed from those of Buddhism. They are Purāṇa Kāśyapa, Māskārin Gośāliputra, Saṃjāyin Vairaṭiputra, Kakuda Kātyāyana, Ajita Keśakambala, and Nirgrantha Jñātiputra.

*six objects for remembrance.* The Buddha, the Law, the order, the precepts, almsgiving, and deities.

*six paramitas (paramitās).* Six practices required of Mahayana bodhisattvas in order to attain Buddhahood. The Sanskrit word *paramita* means "perfection" or "having reached the other shore," that is, having crossed over from the shore of delusion to that of enlightenment. The six practices are: (1) almsgiving, which includes material almsgiving, almsgiving of the Law, and almsgiving of fearlessness; (2) keeping the precepts; (3) forbearance or bearing up patiently under opposition and hardship; (4) assiduousness or diligence in practice; (5) meditation; and (6) wisdom. The

Sanskrit names for the six paramitas are dāna, śīla, kṣānti, vīrya, dhyāna, and prajñā. Sometimes four more are added: (7) skill in expedient means, (8) vows, (9) power, and (10) knowledge, to make ten paramitas.

*six sense-media.* (1) The six sense organs: eyes, ears, nose, tongue, body, and mind. (2) The six sense organs along with their respective objects or things that enter them: form, sound, scent, taste, object, and consciousness.

*six transcendental powers.* Powers that Buddhas, bodhisattvas, and arhats are said to possess. They are: the power of being anywhere at will; the power of seeing anything anywhere; the power of hearing any sound anywhere; the power of knowing the thoughts of all other minds; the power of knowing past lives; and the power of eradicating illusions.

*six types of harmonious respect.* Being harmonious with and respectful of others in action, word, mind, observance of the precepts, doctrine, and religious practice.

*sixty-two erroneous views.* A term denoting all views other than the correct one of selflessness.

*Subhuti (Subhūti).* One of Shakyamuni's ten major disciples, depicted in the Wisdom sutras as foremost in understanding the doctrine of emptiness or nondualism.

*suchness, sometimes called thusness.* The ultimate reality underlying all things, the absolute.

*Sumeru.* A huge mountain that stands at the center of the world. The god Shakra or Indra resides on the top, while the Four Heavenly Kings live halfway down the four sides. At its base are four continents, the most important of which is that lying to the south called Jambudvipa, where Buddhism spreads.

*Tathagata.* See Thus Come One.

*ten evil actions.* See ten good actions.

*ten good actions.* Refraining from committing the ten evil actions, which are: killing, stealing, illicit sexual conduct, lying, harsh words, defaming, duplicity, greed, anger, and the holding of mistaken views.

*ten powers.* The powers of a Buddha, namely, the power of knowing what is true and what is not; the power of knowing the karmic causality at work in the lives of all beings past, present, and future; the power of knowing all stages of concentration, emancipation, and meditation; the power of knowing the life-condition of all people; the power of judging all people's understanding; the power of discerning the superiority or inferiority of all people's capacity; the power of knowing the effects of all people's actions; the power of remembering past lifetimes; the power of knowing when each person will be born and die and in what realm that person will be reborn; and the power of eradicating all illusions.

*thirty-seven elements of the Way.* Thirty-seven practices leading to enlightenment, namely, four states of mindfulness, four types of correct effort, four bases of supernatural power, five roots of goodness, five powers, seven factors of enlightenment, and the eightfold holy path.

*thirty-two features.* Remarkable physical characteristics possessed by great beings such as Buddhas and wheel-turning kings. They are: flat soles; markings of the wheel of the Law on the soles; long slender fingers; broad flat heels; webbed feet and hands; extremely flexible limbs; protuberant insteps; slender legs like those of a deer; hands that extend past the knees even when standing; concealed genitals; body height equal to armspan; body hair that turns upward; one hair growing from each pore; golden skin; light radiating from the body; thin pliant skin; well-developed muscles in hands, feet, shoulders, and nape of neck; well-developed muscles below armpits; dignified torso like that of a lion; large straight body; substantial shoulders; forty teeth; even teeth; four white fangs; full cheeks like those of a lion; unexcelled sense of taste; long broad tongue; voice that can reach to the Brahma heaven; eyes the color of blue lotus blossoms; long eyelashes like those of a cow; protuberant knot of flesh like a topknot on crown of head; tuft of white hair between the eyebrows, curling to the right.

*thousand-millionfold world.* A major world system in ancient Indian cosmology. A world consists of a Mt. Sumeru, its surrounding seas and mountains, heavenly bodies, etc., extending upward to the first meditation heaven in the world of form and downward to the circle of wind that forms the basis of a world. One thousand such worlds make up a minor world system, one thousand minor world systems constitute an intermediate world system, and one thousand intermediate world systems form a major world system. Therefore, one major world system comprises one billion worlds. There were thought to be countless major world systems in the universe.

*three bodies.* An important doctrine in many Mahayana texts, but one that is only touched on in the Vimalakirti Sutra. According to it, the Buddha is viewed as manifesting three aspects or "bodies": (1) the Dharma body (Skt dharma-kāya), the Buddha as the embodiment of the ultimate and unchanging Law or truth; (2) the bliss body or reward body (Skt sambhoga-kāya), the form the Buddha obtained as the reward for completing bodhisattva practice and gaining full enlightenment; and (3) the manifested body (Skt nirmāna-kāya), the physical form in which the Buddha appears in this world in order to save living beings.

*three evils or three evil paths.* The three evil realms of existence, namely, hell, the realm of hungry spirits, and that of beasts.

*Three gates to emancipation.* Emptiness, formlessness, and nonaction or wishlessness.

*three thousand worlds.* Another name for a thousand-millionfold world.

*Three Treasures.* The three things that all Buddhist believers are enjoined to serve and revere, namely, the Buddha, the Law or Dharma, and the Samgha or order.

*three understandings.* Three of the six transcendental powers: the power of seeing anything anywhere, the power of knowing past lives, and the power of eradicating illusions.

158 *three vehicles.* The path or career of the shravaka or voice-hearer; of the pratyekabuddha; and of the bodhisattva or Buddha.

*threefold world.* The world of desire, the world of form, and the world of formlessness. The realms inhabited by unenlightened beings who transmigrate within the six paths. Beings in the world of desire are ruled by various desires. Those in the world of form have material form but no desires. Those in the world of formlessness are free from both desire and form.

*Thus Come One (Skt tathāgata, Ch ju-lai, J nyorai).* One of the ten epithets for a Buddha; a commonly used term for a Buddha.

*Trayastrimsha (Trāyastriṃśa) heaven.* Heaven of the Thirty-Three Gods, second of the six heavens of the world of desire. It is located on a plateau at the top of Mt. Sumeru, where thirty-three gods, including Indra, live. Beings in this heaven have a life span of one thousand years, each day of which is equal to a hundred years in the saha world.

*Tushita (Tuṣita) heaven.* Heaven of Satisfaction, the fourth of the six heavens in the world of desire. It is said that bodhisattvas are reborn there just before their last rebirth in the world when they will attain Buddhahood. The future Buddha, Maitreya, is at present dwelling in the Tushita heaven.

*twelve sense-media.* See six sense-media, definition (2).

*twelve-linked chain of causation.* Also called the doctrine of dependent origination, an important part of the teaching of early Buddhism. It illustrates step by step the causal relationship between ignorance and suffering, i.e., ignorance leads to (karmic) action, action to consciousness, consciousness to name and form, name and form to the six sense organs, the six sense organs to contact, contact to sensation, sensation to desire, desire to attachment, attachment to existence, existence to birth (rebirth), and birth to the sufferings of old age and death.

*Upali (Upāli).* One of Shakyamuni's ten major disciples, known as foremost in observing the precepts.

*voice-hearer (Skt śrāvaka).* One who listens to the teaching of Shakyamuni Buddha. The term originally applied to Shakyamuni's immediate disciples but later came to mean those who follow the teachings of Hinayana Buddhism.

*Vaishali (Vaiśālī).* Large city in northeastern India in the time of Shakyamuni Buddha. Corresponds to the present-day city of Basarh in Bihar.

*wheel-turning king or wheel-turning sage king.* An ideal ruler in Indian mythology. In Buddhism the wheel-turning kings are kings who rule by virtue rather than force.

*yaksha (yakṣa).* A type of demon, one of the eight kinds of nonhuman beings who protect Buddhism.

*yojana.* A unit of measurement in ancient India, equal to the distance that the royal army could march in a day.

## Translations from the Asian Classics

*Major Plays of Chikamatsu*, tr. Donald Keene   1961

*Four Major Plays of Chikamatsu*, tr. Donald Keene. Paperback ed. only.   1961; rev. ed. 1997

*Records of the Grand Historian of China, translated from the Shih chi of Ssu-ma Ch'ien*, tr. Burton Watson, 2 vols.   1961

*Instructions for Practical Living and Other Neo-Confucian Writings by Wang Yang-ming*, tr. Wing-tsit Chan   1963

*Hsün Tzu: Basic Writings*, tr. Burton Watson, paperback ed. only   1963; rev. ed. 1996

*Chuang Tzu: Basic Writings*, tr. Burton Watson, paperback ed. only.   1964; rev. ed. 1996

*The Mahābhārata*, tr. Chakravarthi V. Narasimhan. Also in paperback ed. 1965; rev. ed. 1997

*The Manyōshū*, Nippon Gakujutsu Shinkōkai edition   1965

*Su Tung-p'o: Selections from a Sung Dynasty Poet*, tr. Burton Watson. Also in paperback ed.   1965

*Bhartrihari: Poems*, tr. Barbara Stoler Miller. Also in paperback ed.   1967

*Basic Writings of Mo Tzu, Hsün Tzu, and Han Fei Tzu*, tr. Burton Watson. Also in separate paperback eds.   1967

*The Awakening of Faith, Attributed to Aśvaghosha*, tr. Yoshito S. Hakeda. Also in paperback ed.   1967

*Reflections on Things at Hand: The Neo-Confucian Anthology*, comp. Chu Hsi and Lü Tsu-ch'ien, tr. Wing-tsit Chan   1967

*The Platform Sutra of the Sixth Patriarch*, tr. Philip B. Yampolsky. Also in paperback ed.   1967

162

*Love Song of the Dark Lord: Jayadeva's Gītagovinda,* tr. Barbara Stoler Miller. Also in paperback ed. Cloth ed. includes critical text of the Sanskrit.    1977; rev. ed. 1997

*Ryōkan: Zen Monk-Poet of Japan,* tr. Burton Watson    1977

*Calming the Mind and Discerning the Real: From the Lam rim chen mo of Tson-kha-pa,* tr. Alex Wayman    1978

*The Hermit and the Love-Thief: Sanskrit Poems of Bhartrihari and Bilhaṇa,* tr. Barbara Stoler Miller    1978

*The Lute: Kao Ming's P'i-p'a chi,* tr. Jean Mulligan. Also in paperback ed. 1980

*A Chronicle of Gods and Sovereigns: Jinnō Shōtōki of Kitabatake Chikafusa,* tr. H. Paul Varley    1980

*Among the Flowers: The Hua-chien chi,* tr. Lois Fusek    1982

*Grass Hill: Poems and Prose by the Japanese Monk Gensei,* tr. Burton Watson 1983

*Doctors, Diviners, and Magicians of Ancient China: Biographies of Fang-shih,* tr. Kenneth J. DeWoskin. Also in paperback ed.    1983

*Theater of Memory: The Plays of Kālidāsa,* ed. Barbara Stoler Miller. Also in paperback ed.    1984

*The Columbia Book of Chinese Poetry: From Early Times to the Thirteenth Century,* ed. and tr. Burton Watson. Also in paperback ed. 1984

*Poems of Love and War: From the Eight Anthologies and the Ten Long Poems of Classical Tamil,* tr. A. K. Ramanujan. Also in paperback ed.    1985

*The Bhagavad Gita: Krishna's Counsel in Time of War,* tr. Barbara Stoler Miller    1986

*The Columbia Book of Later Chinese Poetry,* ed. and tr. Jonathan Chaves. Also in paperback ed.    1986

*The Tso Chuan: Selections from China's Oldest Narrative History,* tr. Burton Watson    1989

*Waiting for the Wind: Thirty-six Poets of Japan's Late Medieval Age,* tr. Steven Carter    1989

*Selected Writings of Nichiren,* ed. Philip B. Yampolsky    1990

*Saigyō, Poems of a Mountain Home,* tr. Burton Watson    1990

*The Book of Lieh Tzu: A Classic of the Tao,* tr. A. C. Graham. Morningside ed. 1990

*The Tale of an Anklet: An Epic of South India—The Cilappatikāram of Iḷaṅkō Aṭikaḷ,* tr. R. Parthasarathy    1993

*Waiting for the Dawn: A Plan for the Prince,* tr. and introduction by Wm. Theodore de Bary    1993

*Yoshitsune and the Thousand Cherry Trees: A Masterpiece of the Eighteenth-Century Japanese Puppet Theater,* tr., annotated, and with introduction by Stanleigh H. Jones, Jr.    1993

*The Lotus Sutra,* tr. Burton Watson. Also in paperback ed.    1993

*The Classic of Changes: A New Translation of the I Ching as Interpreted by Wang Bi,* tr. Richard John Lynn    1994

*Beyond Spring: Tz'u Poems of the Sung Dynasty,* tr. Julie Landau    1994

*The Columbia Anthology of Traditional Chinese Literature,* ed. Victor H. Mair 1994

*Scenes for Mandarins: The Elite Theater of the Ming,* tr. Cyril Birch    1995

*Letters of Nichiren,* ed. Philip B. Yampolsky; tr. Burton Watson et al.    1996

*Unforgotten Dreams: Poems by the Zen Monk Shōtetsu,* tr. Steven D. Carter 1997

*The Vimalakirti Sutra,* tr. Burton Watson    1997

*Japanese and Chinese Poems to Sing: The Wakan rōei shū,* tr. J. Thomas Rimer and Jonathan Chaves    1997

*A Tower for the Summer Heat,* Li Yu, tr. Patrick Hanan    1998

*The Classic of the Way and Virtue: A New Translation of the Tao-te ching of Laozi as Interpreted by Wang Bi,* tr. Richard John Lynn    1999

*The Four Hundred Songs of War and Wisdom: An Anthology of Poems from Classical Tamil, The Puranāṇūṟu,* eds. and trans. George L. Hart and Hank Heifetz    1999

*Original Tao: Inward Training (Nei-yeh) and the Foundations of Taoist Mysticism,* by Harold D. Roth    1999

*Lao Tzu's Tao Te Ching: A Translation of the Startling New Documents Found at Guodian,* Robert G. Henricks    2000

# Modern Asian Literature

*Modern Japanese Drama: An Anthology,* ed. and tr. Ted. Takaya. Also in paperback ed.   1979

*Mask and Sword: Two Plays for the Contemporary Japanese Theater,* by
Yamazaki Masakazu, tr. J. Thomas Rimer   1980

*Yokomitsu Riichi, Modernist,* Dennis Keene   1980

*Nepali Visions, Nepali Dreams: The Poetry of Laxmiprasad Devkota,* tr. David
Rubin   1980

*Literature of the Hundred Flowers,* vol. 1: *Criticism and Polemics,* ed. Hualing
Nieh   1981

*Literature of the Hundred Flowers,* vol. 2: *Poetry and Fiction,* ed. Hualing Nieh
1981

*Modern Chinese Stories and Novellas, 1919 1949,* ed. Joseph S. M. Lau, C. T.
Hsia, and Leo Ou-fan Lee. Also in paperback ed.   1984

*A View by the Sea,* by Yasuoka Shōtarō, tr. Kären Wigen Lewis   1984

*Other Worlds; Arishima Takeo and the Bounds of Modern Japanese Fiction,* by
Paul Anderer   1984

*Selected Poems of Sō Chōngju,* tr. with introduction by David R. McCann   1989

*The Sting of Life: Four Contemporary Japanese Novelists,* by Van C. Gessel
1989

*Stories of Osaka Life,* by Oda Sakunosuke, tr. Burton Watson   1990

*The Bodhisattva, or Samantabhadra,* by Ishikawa Jun, tr. with introduction by
William Jefferson Tyler   1990

*The Travels of Lao Ts'an, by Liu T'ieh-yün,* tr. Harold Shadick. Morningside
ed.   1990

*Three Plays by Kōbō Abe,* tr. with introduction by Donald Keene   1993

*The Columbia Anthology of Modern Chinese Literature,* ed. Joseph S. M. Lau
and Howard Goldblatt   1995

*Modern Japanese Tanka,* ed. and tr. by Makoto Ueda   1996

*Masaoka Shiki: Selected Poems,* ed. and tr. by Burton Watson   1997

*Writing Women in Modern China: An Anthology of Women's Literature from
the Early Twentieth Century,* ed. and tr. by Amy D. Dooling and Kristina
M. Torgeson   1998

*American Stories,* by Nagai Kafû, tr. Mitsuko Iriye   2000

## Studies in Asian Culture

*The Ōnin War: History of Its Origins and Background, with a Selective Translation of the Chronicle of Ōnin,* by H. Paul Varley 1967

*Chinese Government in Ming Times: Seven Studies,* ed. Charles O. Hucker 1969

*The Actors' Analects (Yakusha Rongo),* ed. and tr. by Charles J. Dunn and Bungō Torigoe 1969

*Self and Society in Ming Thought,* by Wm. Theodore de Bary and the Conference on Ming Thought. Also in paperback ed. 1970

*A History of Islamic Philosophy,* by Majid Fakhry, 2d ed. 1983

*Phantasies of a Love Thief: The Caurapañatcāśikā Attributed to Bilhaṇa,* by Barbara Stoler Miller 1971

*Iqbal: Poet-Philosopher of Pakistan,* ed. Hafeez Malik 1971

*The Golden Tradition: An Anthology of Urdu Poetry,* ed. and tr. Ahmed Ali. Also in paperback ed. 1973

*Conquerors and Confucians: Aspects of Political Change in Late Yüan China,* by John W. Dardess 1973

*The Unfolding of Neo-Confucianism,* by Wm. Theodore de Bary and the Conference on Seventeenth-Century Chinese Thought. Also in paperback ed. 1975

*To Acquire Wisdom: The Way of Wang Yang-ming,* by Julia Ching 1976

*Gods, Priests, and Warriors: The Bhṛgus of the Mahābhārata,* by Robert P. Goldman 1977

*Mei Yao-ch'en and the Development of Early Sung Poetry,* by Jonathan Chaves 1976

*The Legend of Semimaru, Blind Musician of Japan,* by Susan Matisoff 1977

*Sir Sayyid Ahmad Khan and Muslim Modernization in India and Pakistan,* by Hafeez Malik 1980

*The Khilafat Movement: Religious Symbolism and Political Mobilization in India,* by Gail Minault 1982

*The World of K'ung Shang-jen: A Man of Letters in Early Ch'ing China,* by Richard Strassberg 1983

*The Lotus Boat: The Origins of Chinese Tz'u Poetry in T'ang Popular Culture,*
by Marsha L. Wagner    1984

*Expressions of Self in Chinese Literature,* ed. Robert E. Hegel and Richard C.
Hessney    1985

*Songs for the Bride: Women's Voices and Wedding Rites of Rural India,* by
W. G. Archer; eds. Barbara Stoler Miller and Mildred Archer
1986

*A Heritage of Kings: One Man's Monarchy in the Confucian World,* by
JaHyun Kim Haboush    1988

## Companions to Asian Studies

*Approaches to the Oriental Classics,* ed. Wm. Theodore de Bary    1959

*Early Chinese Literature,* by Burton Watson. Also in paperback ed.    1962

*Approaches to Asian Civilizations,* eds. Wm. Theodore de Bary and Ainslie T.
Embree    1964

*The Classic Chinese Novel: A Critical Introduction,* by C. T. Hsia. Also in paperback ed.    1968

*Chinese Lyricism: Shih Poetry from the Second to the Twelfth Century,* tr.
Burton Watson. Also in paperback ed.    1971

*A Syllabus of Indian Civilization,* by Leonard A. Gordon and Barbara Stoler
Miller    1971

*Twentieth-Century Chinese Stories,* ed. C. T. Hsia and Joseph S. M. Lau. Also
in paperback ed.    1971

*A Syllabus of Chinese Civilization,* by J. Mason Gentzler, 2d ed.    1972

*A Syllabus of Japanese Civilization,* by H. Paul Varley, 2d ed.    1972

*An Introduction to Chinese Civilization,* ed. John Meskill, with the assistance
of J. Mason Gentzler    1973

*An Introduction to Japanese Civilization,* ed. Arthur E. Tiedemann    1974

*Ukifune: Love in the Tale of Genji,* ed. Andrew Pekarik    1982

*The Pleasures of Japanese Literature,* by Donald Keene    1988

*A Guide to Oriental Classics,* eds. Wm. Theodore de Bary and Ainslie T.
Embree; 3d edition ed. Amy Vladeck Heinrich, 2 vols.    1989

## *Introduction to Asian Civilizations*

Wm. Theodore de Bary, Editor

*Sources of Japanese Tradition*, 1958; paperback ed., 2 vols., 1964

*Sources of Indian Tradition*, 1958; paperback ed., 2 vols., 1964; 2d ed., 2 vols., 1988

*Sources of Chinese Tradition*, 1960; paperback ed., 2 vols., 1964; 2d ed., 2 vols., 1999

*Sources of Korean Tradition*, ed. Peter H. Lee and Wm. Theodore de Bary; paperback ed., vol. 1, 1997

*Sources of Chinese Tradition*, 1999; 2d ed., vol. 1, compiled by Wm. Theodore de Bary and Irene Bloom; vol. 2, compiled by Wm. Theodore de Bary and Richard Lufrano

## *Neo-Confucian Studies*

*Instructions for Practical Living and Other Neo-Confucian Writings by Wang Yang-ming*, tr. Wing-tsit Chan    1963

*Reflections on Things at Hand: The Neo-Confucian Anthology*, comp. Chu Hsi and Lü Tsu-ch'ien, tr. Wing-tsit Chan    1967

*Self and Society in Ming Thought*, by Wm. Theodore de Bary and the Conference on Ming Thought. Also in paperback ed.    1970

*The Unfolding of Neo-Confucianism*, by Wm. Theodore de Bary and the Conference on Seventeenth-Century Chinese Thought. Also in paperback ed.    1975

*Principle and Practicality: Essays in Neo-Confucianism and Practical Learning*, eds. Wm. Theodore de Bary and Irene Bloom. Also in paperback ed.    1979

*The Syncretic Religion of Lin Chao-en*, by Judith A. Berling    1980

*The Renewal of Buddhism in China: Chu-hung and the Late Ming Synthesis*, by Chün-fang Yü    1981

*Neo-Confucian Orthodoxy and the Learning of the Mind-and-Heart*, by Wm. Theodore de Bary    1981

*Yüan Thought: Chinese Thought and Religion Under the Mongols,* eds. Hok-
lam Chan and Wm. Theodore de Bary    1982

*The Liberal Tradition in China,* by Wm. Theodore de Bary    1983

*The Development and Decline of Chinese Cosmology,* by John B. Henderson
1984

*The Rise of Neo-Confucianism in Korea,* by Wm. Theodore de Bary and
JaHyun Kim Haboush    1985

*Chiao Hung and the Restructuring of Neo-Confucianism in Late Ming,* by
Edward T. Ch'ien    1985

*Neo-Confucian Terms Explained: Pei-hsi tzu-i,* by Ch'en Ch'un, ed. and trans.
Wing-tsit Chan    1986

*Knowledge Painfully Acquired: K'un-chih chi,* by Lo Ch'in-shun, ed. and trans.
Irene Bloom    1987

*To Become a Sage: The Ten Diagrams on Sage Learning,* by Yi T'oegye, ed. and
trans. Michael C. Kalton    1988

*The Message of the Mind in Neo-Confucian Thought,* by Wm. Theodore de
Bary    1989